How to find and buy a building plot

By Roy Speer and Michael Dade

OVOLO BOOKS
1 THE GRANARY,
BROOK FARM,
ELLINGTON,
HUNTINGDON,
CAMBRIDGESHIRE
PE28 0AE

First edition published 1995 by J M Dent Limited
Second edition published 1998 by Stonepound Books
Third edition published 2010 by Ovolo Books

ISBN 978-1-9059-5932-7

ACKNOWLEDGEMENTS
We thank the following for their help with the book: the late Michael Cheal for supplying plans and illustrations; the individuals who provided case studies; Custom Homes, Oakwrights, Potton and Scandia Hus for the house designs in Chapter 1; Barry Page for the author photos; and the chartered surveyors and estate agents throughout the UK who provided information. .

For more information on Ovolo Books please visit
www.ovolobooks.co.uk
or call 01480 891777 or email: info@ovolobooks.co.uk

How to find and buy a building plot

By Roy Speer and Michael Dade

CONTENTS

FOREWORD

We hope you find this book as useful as have the many people who have contacted us since the first edition of *How to Find and Buy a Building Plot* was published in 1995. It's been fascinating to hear not only of the varied challenges people come across but also of the creativity and determination they've used to overcome those challenges, resulting in many successful building projects. This has helped us revise the book to give you more plot-finding ideas and tips. Many of the readers who contact us do so to find out whether we might be able to help them professionally through our consultancy practice and we have indeed been able to take on some of those cases, helping readers from all over the country. Our office numbers and email addresses are at the end of the book.

The last 14 years has seen the evolution of the internet, which has become a tremendously useful tool in land finding but, don't worry if you're not a computer user, it's still possible to do everything in the traditional ways, it might just take you a little longer. The self-build industry and products have also developed during this period, especially in the help and information now available and in new energy and water saving technology. However, the other main area of change - the planning permission system - hasn't been to the advantage of people like you who want to create their own homes. Government attempts to simplify and streamline the system have, thus far, only served to make it progressively more complicated, obscure and expensive for users. The information you need on planning relevant to plot finding is contained in this book but the companion title, *How to Get Planning Permission*, provides the detail on making planning applications.

Whatever type of house or conversion you're proposing, we wish you success with your search, purchase and building project.

Roy Speer & Mike Dade
April 2010

INTRODUCTION

Many people dream of building their own home. For some it's a way of acquiring an ideal home, for others it's an economical means of providing accommodation, or even a way of making money. Every year thousands of people do build their own homes, or have one built specifically for them. The way they go about this - the amount of work they do, how the house is designed, the type of construction, where their finance comes from - varies slightly in every case. One of the few things all of them have in common, though, is finding a suitable piece of land on which to build their house - probably the biggest single challenge they face. Yet good practical and informed advice is scarce and, until the first edition of *How to Find and Buy a Building Plot* was published 1995, there was no comprehensive source of information on how to find and buy land on which to build a house. This book was originally written to fill that gap.

If you plan to find and buy an existing building to convert into a new home,

rather than to build a new house from scratch, most of the advice in this book is equally relevant. For simplicity's sake, we shall refer in the text just to 'building plots', but you should read this phrase to encompass conversion properties as well.

Some people build a home for themselves in the garden of their existing house. They're fortunate, as they only have to worry about planning permission, service connections, ground conditions and legal and planning restrictions, unlike the rest who face the additional hurdles of finding a plot - a rare commodity in many areas - and completing a purchase, often in the face of stiff competition. This book covers all these points and most of the content is as relevant to people who have a plot in their garden, as it is to those who don't.

For convenience, we'll frequently refer to a building plot-buyer as a 'self-builder' in the text, but this has a very wide meaning here. The book is intended for anyone who wants to buy a plot or build a house or convert an existing building. The information and advice apply whether you intend to build a house yourself, or have one built for you, or whether you're a builder or a professional, advising others.

The book is based on current law, regulations and practice in England. Apart from property law in Scotland, these are broadly similar throughout the UK. There are differences in detail and terminology between the countries and we draw attention to some of these in the text. Rules and regulations do change over time. For these reasons, it's vital to double check crucial details – such as time limits and precise procedural requirements – before taking action. A book isn't a substitute for specific advice on your particular circumstances.

How to Find and Buy a Building Plot is arranged in five Parts, each dealing with a main stage in the process. Defining requirements should be the starting point. This is often overlooked by people eager to press ahead but who often come to grief later. Finding a plot involves looking in the usual places where plots are sold and sometimes, through necessity, in less obvious places. Having found a plot, you need to assess it to make sure that it meets your requirements with no hidden pitfalls that could add unexpected cost or even prevent you building. The book then turns to the key question of how much a plot is worth before looking at how to buy a plot successfully. It ends with some self-builders' case histories showing how three families found and bought their sites.

PART 1

DEFINING YOUR REQUIREMENTS

Your first step towards finding and buying a building plot should be to work out your requirements - size and design of house, amount of land, location and how much you can afford to spend. You need specific answers to these questions before you start looking. Buyers who define their requirements precisely and have their finance already arranged are well placed to secure a plot. Estate agents and banks or building societies don't take seriously people who seem vague about what they plan to do.

CHAPTER 1
THE HOUSE

House building is about creating a new home so we'll start by considering the building itself. Usually the biggest constraint here is the budget which we deal with in Chapter 4. In practice, you'll probably have to adjust both your budget and your dream home several times in order to match the two. Whether you already have ideas about your ideal home or have a completely open mind, you need to pin your ideas down and define your requirements precisely.

DESIGN IDEAS

A good way to settle on a design is to find ideas from plans and photographs of finished houses. There's a wealth of information available to help you. The various magazines about self-build and home improvement, such as Build It, Grand Designs, Homebuilding and Renovating and Self Build and Design, carry advertisements for self-build package companies and many of these have websites and catalogues packed with plans and photographs. In addition, the

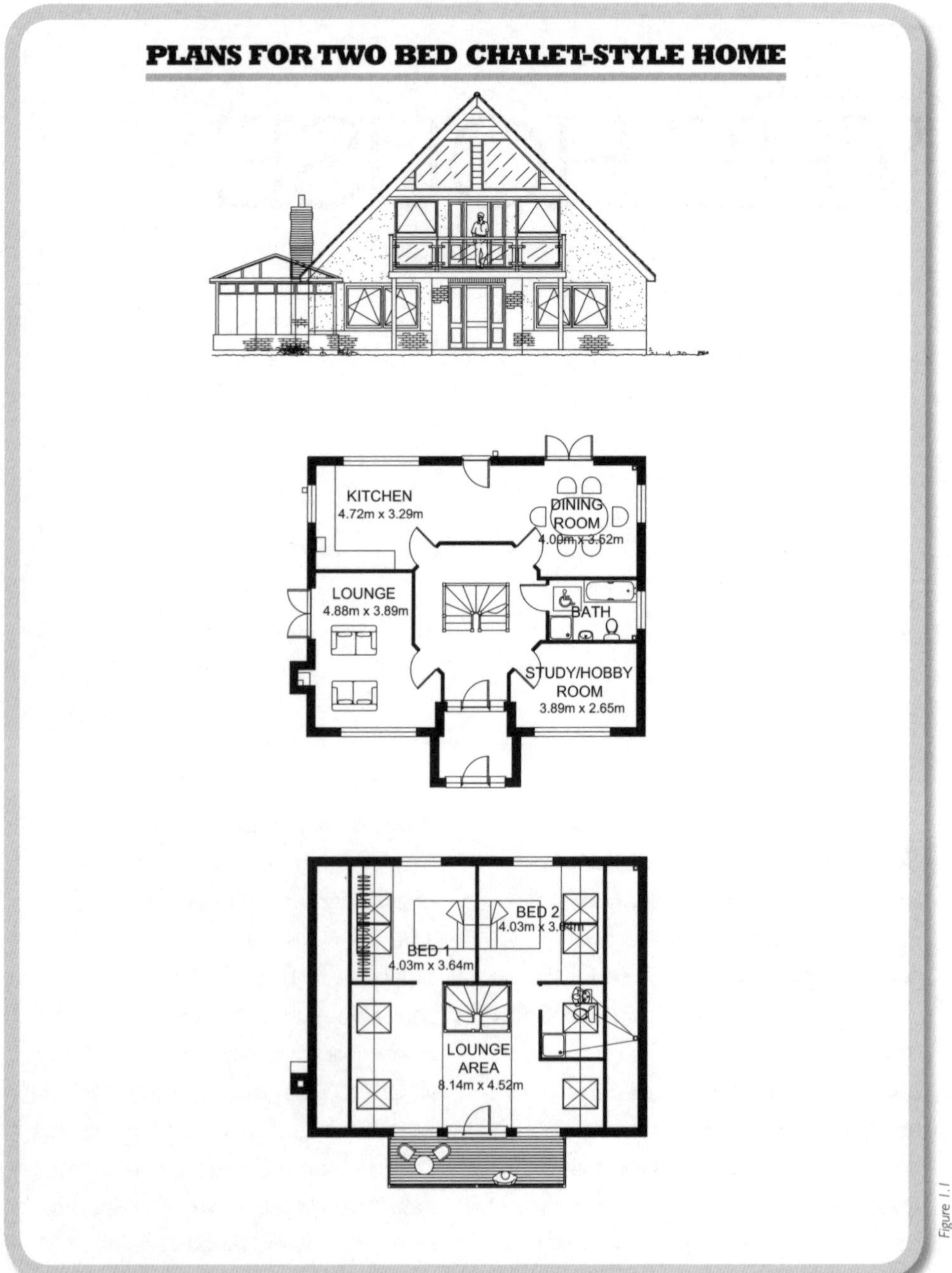

Custom Homes' Seahaven two-bedroom chalet 197 sq m

magazines publicise the many shows and exhibitions which take place each year. Exhibitions provide an opportunity to gather ideas and to gain an impression of the companies behind the brochures and advertisements. Major shows often feature a show house built for the occasion and walking around it is a good way of focusing your mind on what you do and don't like. The National Self Build and Renovation Centre at Swindon is a permanent exhibition that also stages regular shows and events.

If you can't visit a self-build show, there might be a show house in a new housing development nearby. Failing that, estate agents have recently-built houses on their books that you can view. During your visit, take notes, measurements and photographs. You can also pick up ideas from any existing house – family members', friends' and neighbours' homes and, indeed, any properties you visit or happen to see on your travels.

Several useful books are available containing hundreds of house plans. Use these for inspiration and to help direct your thinking. By these means, your eventual design will be born out of your personal preferences, which might not be catered for in a standard design.

TV programmes about house building, renovation and conversion are now a staple of many channels from which you can gain an insight into different styles, layouts and materials and construction options from the comfort of your armchair. This can broaden your horizons but won't replace the experience of seeing things in the flesh.

PROFESSIONAL ADVICE

Designing houses is complex and you will almost certainly need to consult a professional at some point. Drawing up detailed plans before you find a plot could mean time and money wasted, as your design should be based on the constraints and opportunities of an actual site. An informal chat with a professional before you start can help define your requirements.

You can get advice from self-build package companies or from independent consultants, such as building surveyors, architectural technologists or architects (to whom we'll refer collectively as 'building designers'). Most of the self-build package companies offer flexibility in their designs and some employ professionals who can help you choose the right design.

PLANS FOR FOUR-BEDROOM HOUSE

Figure 1.2

Concept 3, a four-bedroom house from Potton's Zenit range 198 sq m

However, don't forget that they work for the company and could be restricted by the particular packages and options it offers. Alternatively, you can pay for independent professional advice.

The best way to find a suitable design professional is by referral. Ask friends, colleagues and other professional advisers about any building designers they've used, look online or in Yellow Pages or similar directory. Check for professional qualifications: MRICS means Chartered Surveyor; ARIBA, Chartered Architect; TechRICS, Surveying Technician; MCIAT, Architectural Technologist; MBEng, Building Engineer. How ever you find a building designer, establish that he or she's right for the job and whether his or her likes or dislikes match yours. Ask to see plans and photos of previous projects and where you can see some houses that have been built. Speak to other clients. Don't only ask if they were pleased with the end result. Ask if the building designer was easy to contact, how quickly he responded and did what he was asked, and whether he had good relations with council building inspectors and planning officers. Once you're satisfied that this is the right person for the job, brief him fully on your requirements and your budget. Agree precisely the work to be done and the fee. Get written confirmation of the figures and when payments are due.

DETAILED REQUIREMENTS

Once you've some ideas, turn them into more specific requirements. Think about the size of the house in terms of the number and dimensions of rooms. The number of bedrooms and the amount of space needed for cooking, eating and living depend on the size of your family and how often you have guests. Consider your requirements now and for the future. Do you have an expanding family or will you need a granny annexe? Think about your lifestyle. Do you entertain frequently? If so, a good-sized dining and living room are a must, complemented with an adequate hall and cloakroom. Perhaps you'd like a state of the art kitchen integral to your dining area to show off your culinary skills. Outdoor types might need plenty of space for wellies and dogs so that a utility room next to the back door could be essential. Hobbies might need extra space, such as a darkroom, library or gym. If you work from home,

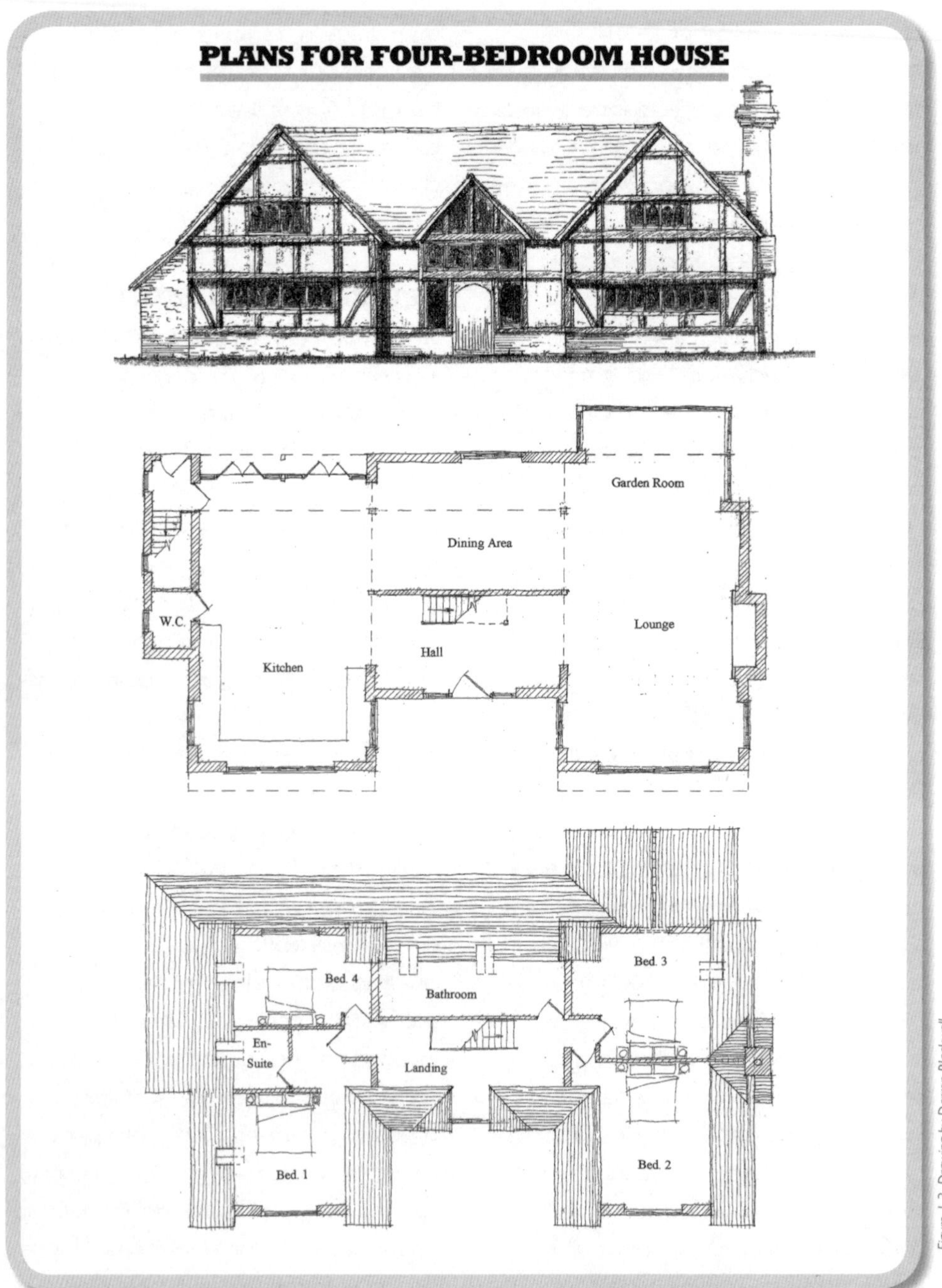

The Lavington by Oakwrights four bedroom house 312 sq m

you might need an office. Modern houses rarely have cellars, although they provide useful additional space for more than wine, but they can be expensive to build. Similarly, since you'll be building a roof, why not make the attic space useable.

Consider the garage at an early stage. Its size will depend on its use - for storing lawn mowers, spare furniture, or as a workshop - sometimes even for parking cars. If your pride and joy is a 1950s Cadillac, it might not fit in to a standard-sized garage. Councils often try to restrict the amount of parking space so, if you want a lot of garaging, you might have to justify this. The fact that you own half a dozen cars might not sway the council if it has such a policy.

Finally, don't worry too much at this stage about how the layout will work. It's tempting to become distracted by design details, but this can lead you to overlook basic requirements.

HOUSE TYPES

Detached houses fall into three main types: house, bungalow and chalet bungalow (see Figures 1.1 to 1.4). The term 'chalet bungalow' means a two-storey building with upper rooms within, or partly within, the roof. Chalets have dormer windows or roof lights at first-floor level, and the ridge of the roof is generally lower than in traditional two-storey houses. The distinction between houses and chalets is often blurred. It's worth bearing in mind that you can sometimes build a chalet-type house on a plot originally intended for a bungalow, where you wouldn't be able to build a full two-storey house. You can normally build a chalet on a plot intended for a house, so the choice of plot is greater if you opt for a chalet-style rather than either a house or bungalow. Occasionally opportunities arise to build 'attached' new houses, adding a new unit onto the end of a terrace or perhaps turning a pair of semis into a three-house terrace. Here your house type is likely to be the same as whatever you're building on to, which in most cases would be a two-storey house.

LAYOUT OPTIONS

When you've worked out in broad terms what accommodation and type of house you want, you need to achieve a workable layout. Think how you would use the house. You might not want a study next to a playroom, or guests moving from living room to dining room via the kitchen, but you might need a spare bedroom on the ground floor if elderly relatives stay. Outline ideas are all you need at this stage. Ultimately, you'll probably work with a building designer or self-build package company to achieve an ideal layout or perhaps find one 'off the peg'.

Try sketching your outline ideas on paper. This helps you to calculate the floor area of the house accurately. The example plan and calculations show how this is done (see Figures 1.5 and 1.6). You now have a rough floor area for your house, but this omits the area of internal walls. For most purposes, floor area is calculated as the area enclosed by the internal surfaces of the external walls, so round up your rough calculation to reflect this.

Floor area is an essential tool in working out the build cost, and can form the basis for discussions with a building designer or self-build package company. When sketching ideas, remember the stairs. Having fitted them into the ground floor plan, work out where they'd emerge upstairs. In a chalet-style house, stairs must avoid sloping ceilings to provide enough headroom. You also need to allow for functional space for fitted wardrobes, cupboards, airing cupboard, boiler, etc. Think about the garage: it could be integral (built into the house), possibly with first-floor rooms above; it could be attached at the side, front or even back of the house or completely detached.

The design and layout of your house is a matter of personal preference, tempered by practical constraints. Getting value for money and securing planning permission are two hurdles which can trip the more adventurous. Compared with traditional building forms, unusual houses can cost more to build and appeal to a smaller market. If you favour contemporary design, the good news is that councils are now more attuned to this, although you still need to pick the right spot to make your bold architectural statement.

The best way to arrive at your ideal design is to work from the inside outwards. Think about the quality of living space you want: light and airy, or warm and cosy; a cottagey feel, or something more formal. Such general points influence matters like ceiling heights and the size, shape and numbers of windows. For the external appearance of the house there's a wide choice of design and

Figure 1.4

Scandia Hus' Bornholm three-bedroom bungalow 156 sq m

materials. In practice, your choice might be limited, as not every design is suitable for every site. This is something councils take into account when deciding whether to give planning permission. Planning permission is a vital element in buying a building plot which we look at in Part Three. For design purposes bear in mind that styles and materials vary across the country. A stone house with a slate roof can look out of place in a village built of bricks and clay tiles. Final decisions on design will ultimately be influenced by the location and surroundings of your plot. By all means have an ideal, but keep one or two alternative ideas to hand. An over-rigid approach will restrict the number of plots that meet your requirements.

	width x depth	sq m	(sq ft)
Ground floor			
Kitchen	3.25 x 4.25	13.80	(149)
Dining room	3.75 x 3.15	11.80	(127)
Sitting room	4.00 x 6.20	24.80	(267)
Utility room	2.60 x 2.55	6.60	(71)
WC	1.00 x 2.55	2.50	(27)
Hall/stairs		2.00	(129)
Total ground floor		71.50	(770)
First floor			
Bedroom 1	4.00 x 6.20		
less	1.70 x 2.00	21.40	(230)
Bedroom 2	3.75 x 3.15	11.80	(127)
Bedroom 3	3.75 x 2.55	9.60	(103)
Bedroom 4	3.25 x 2.30	7.50	(80)
En suite	2.55 x 2.00	5.10	(55)
Bathroom	2.00 x 1.8	3.60	39)
Landing stairs		13.00	(140)
Total first floor		71.50	(770)
Total internal floor area		143.00	(1,540)

ORGANISING CONSTRUCTION

Your chosen way of carrying out the project will have a bearing on the cost of the house and its design and, ultimately, on finding and buying the right plot. The options fall into five broad categories:

- building-designer-led project: the designer co-ordinates and oversees the project, from preparing the plans to supervising the build
- complete design and build package, also known as a 'turn-key' package: a specialist company undertakes the entire project, sometimes including site-finding and buying
- project management package: a project manager organises and oversees the build on your behalf

self-managed, labour sub-contracted: you manage the project, hiring and co-ordinating sub-contractors to do all the building work

- self-managed, self-build: you do everything, acting as both builder and project manager

These aren't clear-cut categories and self-builders often use a combination to complete their projects. As a general rule, the more work you do yourself, the cheaper the build will be. This might release more money for a bigger or better plot. The greater your own involvement in the construction or its supervision, the more accessible you must be to the site. Trying to co-ordinate several teams of sub-contractors by phone is unlikely to produce the desired results in the right time. However, accessibility might narrow your area of search making it harder to find a plot.

HOW TO CALCULATE ROOM SIZES AND WORK OUT FLOOR AREA

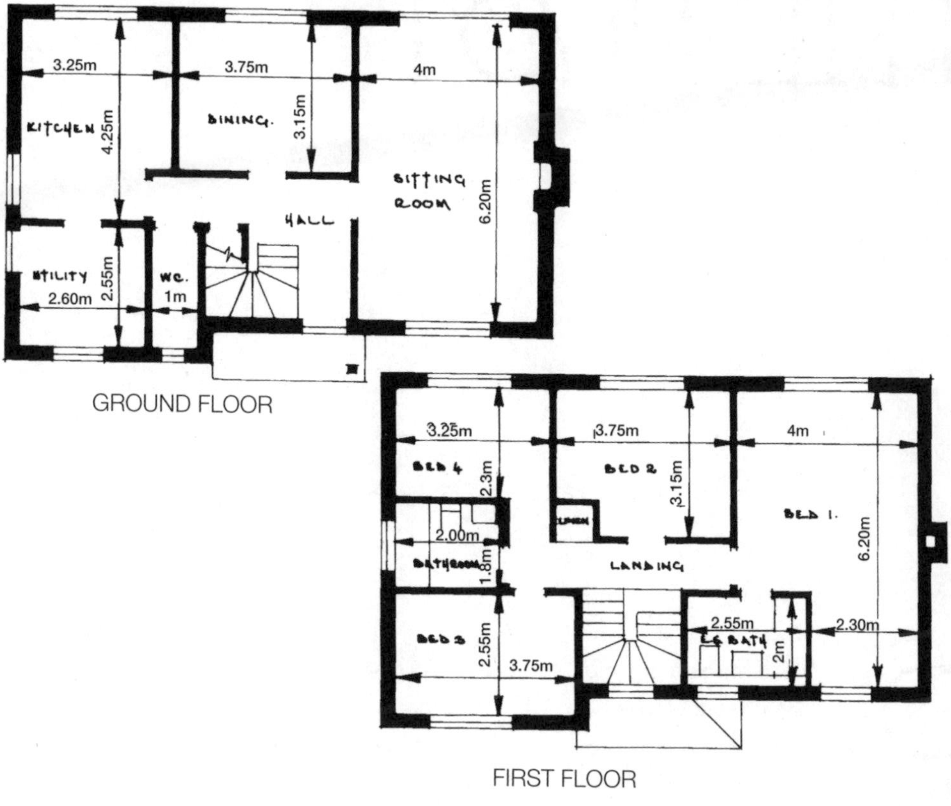

GROUND FLOOR

FIRST FLOOR

Figures 1.5 & 1.6

CONSTRUCTION METHODS

Most houses were traditionally built of timber frame or brick and block, although reinforced concrete, steel frame, structural insulated panel (SIPs) and various other forms of construction now available are equally viable alternatives. Cost, speed of build, flexibility of design and thermal efficiency are some of the factors to consider in choosing which method to use. The type of construction is unlikely to affect your choice of plot and won't be considered when you apply for planning permission.

CHAPTER 2

THE PLOT

Once you've an idea of what you want to build, think about the building plot. Your plot might have to accommodate:

- house
- garage
- access drive and turning area
- garden
- outbuildings

SIZE OF PLOT

The size of house and, possibly, garage determines the minimum width or 'frontage' of the plot. Allow at least 1 m (3ft 3ins) between the sides of the house and each boundary for maintenance of walls, gutters and roof. You can build foundations right up to a boundary but this might create a maintenance problem, as you couldn't maintain the wall, gutter or roof, without going onto neighbouring land. You might also meet resistance from the council if you try to squeeze your house into too tight a space, as the Building Regulations impose minimum wall-to-boundary distances, especially where the wall has windows and doors. In most situations, the minimum

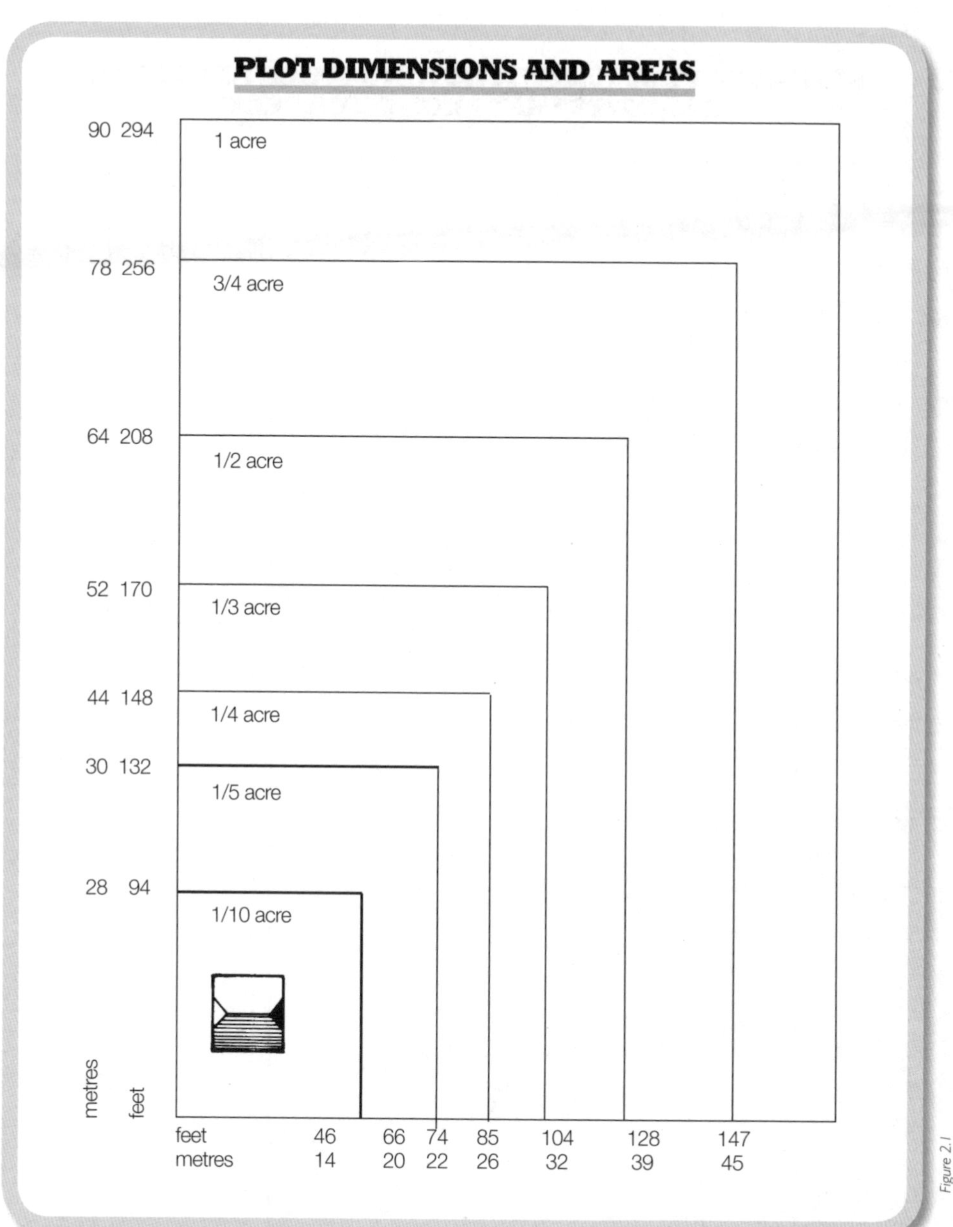

Figure 2.1

plot frontage you need, then, is the width of the house, plus the width of the garage, plus at least 3 m (10 ft). Also allow a gap between the house and the garage. On some plots a detached garage in front of

HALF ACRE PLOT (0.2HA) SHOWING SPACE NEEDED FOR ELEMENTS THAT MIGHT BE NEEDED

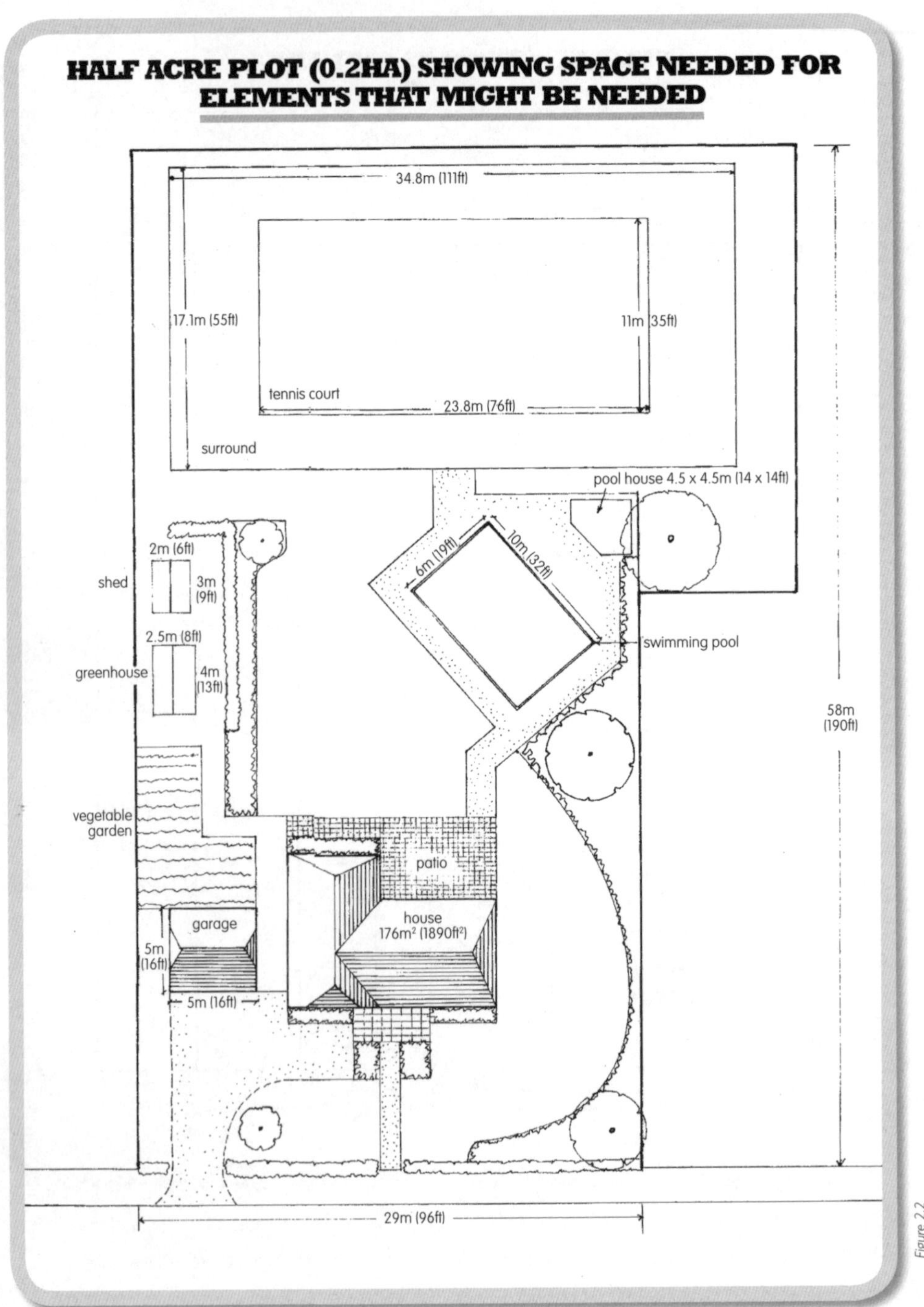

Figure 2.2

the house is suitable. This allows a narrower plot, but can spoil views from front windows. An alternative for a narrow plot is an integral garage. Councils' parking standards for new houses generally require at least one off-street parking space. For a family-sized house, ideally allow two spaces (probably in the garage) plus enough space for children's and visitors' cars. In towns, councils might try to restrict the number of parking spaces as part of their efforts to reduce reliance on cars for transport. Speak to the council to find out its requirements.

The type of road to which your plot has access might mean you have to provide an on-site turning area so that cars don't have to back out into traffic. This is essential for plots on major or through roads. Access without a turning area is usually allowed only in a cul-de-sac or no-through-road. Turning areas require space which has to be allowed for in your plot. Access, an important and potentially complex matter, is fully explained in Part Three.

The size of garden you need depends on how you plan to use it. Do you entertain in the garden, play games or sports, or grow fruit and vegetables? A gardening enthusiast might want greenhouses and potting sheds. Other requirements can include space for patio, workshop, conservatory, play equipment, swimming pool or tennis court. You might need to allow for trees, shrubs and fences to provide privacy. Don't overlook functional areas like washing lines, dustbins, and compost bins - all take up space. If you keep horses you might want a paddock. Note that a '3.75 acre plot' and a '0.75 acre plot plus 3 acre paddock' are very different. A 3.75 acre plot could offer scope for a very large house which will be priced accordingly. A 0.75 acre plot plus paddock is just that - the paddock probably couldn't be built on or incorporated in the garden, although an adjoining paddock will add to the price of the plot.

Once you've a clear idea of your requirements for the outside, calculate the area and frontage of the plot you need to accommodate them (see Figure 2.1). A sketch plan (see Figure 2.2) will be helpful and more so if you draw it to scale. A scale of 1:200 is fairly straightforward: each metre on the ground is represented by half a centimetre on the page. A plan may seem unnecessary at this stage, but is useful when you come to work out whether your house will actually fit a particular plot.

PLOT CHARACTERISTICS

Plots come in all shapes and sizes

Figure 2.3

The site of three garages makes an urban infill plot in a dense built-up area

and not all the parts can necessarily be used. An irregular shape, steeply sloping ground or the presence of trees or other obstacles, might mean that you need a larger total area than your initial calculations suggest. The character of plots varies from small urban infill sites to acres of isolated countryside (see Figures 2.3 and 2.4). Plots can be individual, part of a small group, or part of an estate of new houses. A coastal plot could be little more than a patch of shingle, a rural plot could be overgrown woodland, and an urban plot could be occupied by dilapidated buildings. Many plots are created from existing large gardens where established trees and hedges add instant character and reduce landscaping costs. They can, however, add to building costs and restrict the choice of site layout. The opposite extreme, bare land, might need extensive landscaping but it's straightforward to lay out and build.

The land may be level or steeply sloping. Often, because of ill-defined or overgrown boundaries, it's hard to see a plot there at all. Sometimes sites look deceptively small, just as

Figure 2.4

A garden plot at the end of a long garden with rear access in a residential area

the footprint of a house does when pegged out on the ground. Whatever the existing character of the plot, you'll change it radically with your house, drive, access and garden. Ultimately it's you who shapes the character of your plot.

Definite ideas on the size, location and character of plot you want are an invaluable aid to finding the right site but, as with house design, it doesn't pay to be too rigid in your thinking. Many people start with unrealistic expectations of what their money will buy, so look at plots for sale and plots where new houses have been built. New detached houses on estates marketed with 'generous' or 'spacious' gardens rarely occupy more than a fifth of an acre, yet this accommodates an 1,800 sq ft (176 sq m) house, double garage and garden. Be wary of agents' descriptions of plot sizes: 'about 0.5 acre', can turn out to be nearer one third of an acre, despite the Property Misdescriptions Act of 1991. Increasingly, though, adverts for plots are giving the precise area in square metres, which is a helpful innovation.

CHAPTER 3

THE LOCATION

There's an old saying in the property business that the three most important factors in assessing land are: location, location and location. This is true of building plots.

You can change a site by landscaping and by adding or removing buildings, homes can be extended, decorated, given a new cladding, or even pulled down and rebuilt in a different style but the location of a plot is permanent.

Building your own home involves: arranging finance; buying a plot; choosing a house; obtaining planning permission and building regulations approval; and then building and fitting out. The process involves an enormous commitment of time, energy and money so it's vitally important that you invest this in the right location. Don't wait until the house is complete before finding out that there's an hour's drive to the nearest school, that buses don't run from the places where your family and friends live, or that it's down wind from a pig farm.

Figure 3.1

A demolished garage and side garden form a suburban plot on a 1950s housing estate

THE COUNTRYSIDE

Plots are found wherever there are opportunities to get planning permission to build - from town centres to deepest countryside. Modern planning regulations date from 1948 and, prior to that, development occurred in a much more piecemeal fashion. Local and national planning policies now dictate that new housing in the countryside is strictly limited. 'Countryside', for planning purposes, is all land outside the limits of cities, towns and villages, as defined in councils' Local Plans and Local Development Frameworks. This means that rural hamlets, small villages and suburban fringes can be classified as 'countryside', even where they comprise large amounts of housing and other buildings.

Opportunities do, though, exist in the countryside, perhaps to replace a derelict house or where an old planning permission has been kept alive over the years. In very limited circumstances, operators of agricultural and other rural businesses can gain planning permission to build houses and this is dealt with in Chapter 12. Some rural plots can be subject to an 'agricultural tie', restricting occupation of the house to someone working in or retired from agriculture.

TOWNS AND VILLAGES

Inside towns and larger villages, council planning policies generally allow new housing. Available plots are more common in areas of sparse or irregular housing on the edge of towns. Victorian houses with very large gardens provide opportunities for infilling. Small houses on big plots offer scope for replacement houses or sub-division. Paddocks and orchards within or adjoining towns also provide opportunities for plots. Areas of large-scale new development can also yield single plots as developers and councils sometimes sell individual plots to self-builders. These can be re-development sites in town centres or greenfield sites on the edge of towns. Commercial sites, especially in or near residential areas, can get planning permission for building plots. These include former garages and pubs, builder's yards, small factories and nursery gardens. In town centres there's scope to convert buildings or space above shops, to replace or extend buildings, including adding floors or excavating basements.

AREA OF SEARCH

Finding the location that's right for you involves first defining the area where you want to live. You can then concentrate your search within that area for plots that meet your practical and aesthetic requirements, from which you can make a final choice. Defining your area of search demands a careful examination of all aspects of your life. Factors that influence the choice of location can include: where your friends and family live; where you've lived previously; where you work; your type of work; whether you have children at school; where shopping, social and leisure facilities are; and access to road, rail and airport links. Consider each in terms of travelling time. From this, a pattern should emerge and you can begin to define an area. Plot these key locations on a map (see Figure 3.3). Don't necessarily just draw a circle around one point, say, a ten-mile radius of your optimum location as the area which meets all your requirements will probably be irregularly shaped. Exclude all locations where you definitely don't want to live. Draw your area of search as widely as possible to give yourself maximum scope - in areas of short supply, some plot-buyers end up settling for a different county from

Figure 3.2

Plots in the countryside are relatively rare but a gap between houses can sometimes become a rural infill plot

the one in which they started looking.

If you want to live in the countryside and nowhere else, your choice is going to be restricted compared with a buyer who'll also accept town or village locations. If you've very particular requirements, like a river frontage or a spectacular view, your choice will be restricted still further. To increase your choice of plots, widen your area of search. Your quest for the right site could, however, distance you from family, friends, or schools. Consequently, a thorough analysis of your priorities is essential to define a realistic area of search.

INFLUENCES ON CHOICE

Keep in mind the geography of the area and the surrounding uses. High ground can be windy or liable to snow or fog. Low-lying ground can flood or, again, be windy if it's open and exposed. A plot near the coast might be appealing in summer but bleak and miserable in winter. Motorways and airports are noisy, and even rural roads can become choked with

Get a map of the area and mark on it all the places where you would want to live to make an area of search plan to use as the basis for your property hunting and to brief estate agents and others on your requirements

holiday traffic in summer. A lively seaside town may be dead out-of-season. Industry, power stations, and rubbish tips could have noise, health and traffic implications. Even an idyllic rural area might suffer from agricultural noise and smell or, on the other hand, be so quiet as to create a sense of isolation in those used to urban bustle.

Advice on plot-hunting sometimes emphasises the need to compromise and be realistic in your expectations. Be realistic by all means, but don't take this too far. If there are few plots available in your area of search, you might either have to accept a long wait for the right plot, or compromise on your requirements. If your enjoyment of your dream home will be constantly marred by the roar of traffic from a main road, wait for a quieter plot elsewhere. Also, your willingness to compromise might depend on how long you plan to live in the house.

Finally, think about the social implications of your chosen location as not every community welcomes outsiders with open arms. This only applies in a small number of cases, but if you don't know the area already, find out about it before buying a plot there.

Having looked at the factors that influence where you want to live, keep in mind the cost and availability of plots as prices vary enormously across Britain. The budget for a two-bedroom bungalow on a small but select plot in Surrey might stretch to a four-bedroom house with several acres of unspoilt countryside in the Western Isles of Scotland.

CHAPTER 4

THE BUDGET

How do you know what you can afford to spend on a building plot? To answer this vital question you need to work out a budget covering the purchase of the plot and the construction of the house itself. When you start looking for plots and when the time comes to make an offer, you must be certain about how much you can afford and that the money will be available when it's needed. Of course, until you find a plot you can't be certain about basic details like final design or foundation costs. Nevertheless, prepare a draft budget like the one in Figure 4.1 at this stage and you can firm it up as your plans progress. This is time well spent as overspending on the perfect plot might put building your dream home financially out of reach.

THE DRAFT BUDGET

There are three basic elements in a draft budget:

- cost of the build
- cost of the plot
- available finance

Clearly, the first two figures must total less than the third for your

DRAFT BUDGET TO WORK OUT COSTS

1 Calculating the total fund required to buy a plot and build your house

Plot price, including fees	120,000
Estimated building costs, including contingency	200,000
Total funds required	£320,000

2 Calculating what size house you can afford to build

Maximum amount of funds available	320,000
Plot price, including fees	(120,000)
	£200,000
Allow for building cost @ £1,000 per sq m	
Maximum size of house in sq m (£200,000/1000) =	200 sq m

3 Calculating how much you can afford to spend on a plot

Maximum amount of funds available	320,000
Estimated building costs, including contingency	(200,000)
Maximum amount available for plot and fees	£120,000

Figure 4.1

Prepare a draft budget to work out how much money you will need to spend on elements of the project

project to be viable. If you know roughly the size of house you want to build, you can work out an approximate build cost. You can find out the level of plot prices in the area of your search. Add these figures to estimate the amount of money you have to find. Alternatively, look at the equation the other way round. From the finance available, deduct the build cost to arrive at the sum you can spend on a plot. Your draft budget can start life on the back of an envelope as a guesstimate of what you can afford. To pin down more precisely how much money you can spend on a plot, or what size house you can afford to build, look more closely at each of the main elements.

FINANCE OPTIONS

First, look at your total available finance. This is normally made up of:

- the equity in your existing house (value of the house less any outstanding mortgage)
- any capital you or your family have available
- the amount you can raise by a new mortgage or loan

TYPICAL CONSTRUCTION COSTS OF NEW HOMES

Example 1

Bungalow, three bedrooms, 150 sq m (1,600 sq ft), brick and block, double garage, owner doing all building work

Preliminaries	9,000
Foundations	5,000
Outside walls	12,000
Roof (structure and covering)	8,250
Inside walls	5,250
Finishes	5,700
Joinery and iron mongery	7,500
Plumbing and heating system	6,000
Electrics	9,500
Decoration	3,300
Total building cost	71,500

Example 2

Chalet, three bedrooms, 165 sq m (1,800 sq ft), timber frame, double garage, owner doing some building work

Preliminaries	9,150
Foundations	8,000
Outside walls	47,850
Roof (structure and covering)	13,500
Inside walls	6,750
Finishes	7,400
Joinery and iron mongery	12,850
Plumbing and heating system	13,500
Electrics	9,500
Decoration	4,500
Total building cost	133,000

In assessing remaining equity in your existing house don't forget to deduct costs of sale - agents' commission, solicitors' fees and removal expenses. Take account of market conditions, be realistic about how much your house will fetch and remember that asking prices aren't necessarily selling prices. Check your estimate with local estate agents who are usually happy to give a valuation in the hope of gaining your instructions when the time comes to sell.

If you're adding any capital into the budget, get advice on the most tax-efficient way to use it and what proportion to put in.

Example 3

Two storey, four bedrooms, 185 sq m (2,000 sq ft), brick and block, double garage, owner doing no building work

Preliminaries	13,000
Foundations	13,900
Outside walls	36,000
Roof (structure and covering)	27,750
Inside walls	16,650
Finishes	19,500
Joinery and iron mongery	27,000
Plumbing and heating system	20,000
Electrics	16,750
Decoration	9,450
Total building cost	200,000

Figure 4.2

Where you need to take out a new mortgage or loan, look at all the options, as there are now many different schemes and your individual circumstances will determine which is the most suitable. The main sources of finance for building your own home are banks and building societies. Most are fully aware of self-build and able to offer help and advice either through their branches or a specialist self-build finance department. Some offer finance packages aimed at people building their own homes, others devise a specific scheme tailor-made for your needs.

Most lenders expect you to put your equity in at the start of the project to fund or part fund the plot purchase. The lender then makes staged payments to cover the construction work. In the past some self-build some mortgage deals allowed people to stay in their existing house while the new house was being built. This is now very rare, although one or two lenders might still consider such an arrangement where a current mortgage is low and the equity input is high. In most cases, therefore, when you locate a suitable plot, your lender is likely to expect you to sell your existing house before making the finance available. Each lender has its own lending criteria, so check the small print carefully. Points to look for include:

- restrictions on the 'age' of the planning permission on the plot - a permission that expires within a year or two might not be acceptable
- restrictions on the start and finish dates of your build
- stage payments during the build -

check whether the lender's stages tie in with the stages at which your builder or package company needs to be paid

- restrictions on who builds, the type of structural warranty and provisions for insurance

Whatever your situation, a chat with your bank, building society or financial adviser is a good starting point to sort out your method of finance but do shop around for the best deal for your particular circumstances.

BUILD COST

The next step is to look more closely at the build cost (see Figure 4.2). Get a rough figure, based on a price per square metre or square foot, from a builder, building designer or self-build package company. A very useful book on construction and building costs is The House Builder's Bible by Mark Brinkley. Self-build magazines and self-build package companies' brochures give indications of current price levels. These are a good starting point, but you must check how the figures are made up - whether they include: professional fees; cost of service connections; foundations; garage; drive, fencing and landscaping; or insurance. Budgets for kitchens and bathrooms can be modest. Brochures include rough costings based on ideal scenarios - a level, serviced plot; good soil conditions; existing access; and fenced boundaries - but you might not be so lucky. Add any missing elements plus a contingency figure of at least 5 per cent to cover any unforeseen expenses.

You'll pay VAT on building materials although in most cases you can claim this back when the project is complete. Make sure that VAT is accounted for in your budget because, even if you can get the VAT back, there's still a significant impact on your cash flow in the meantime.

PLOT PRICE

For a rough idea of the likely cost of a building plot, look at on-line plot finding services to see asking prices. Better still, contact estate agents in the area of your search. Tell them what type of house you want to build and the sort of location you're looking for. They can tell you what plots are actually selling for, as opposed to just the asking price. If you already have a builder, building designer or self-build package company, they might be able to give you an indication of current price levels for plots. Self-build magazines contain lists of land for sale with asking prices and sometimes indicative figures for plots around the United Kingdom and Northern Ireland.

ADJUSTING THE FIGURES

Once you have preliminary figures for plot and building costs, compare these with the amount of money you've got available for the project. If the figures look tight at this stage, think about the implications. Your estimated build costs are more likely to increase than decrease as the project progresses. Examine your priorities carefully. If a particular house-type is your overriding priority, cost this accurately and then see what's left for the plot. Consider whether that figure will buy a plot of adequate size in the right location. If it won't, decide whether you're prepared to look further afield or to spend the additional time and effort finding the right plot at a bargain price. Alternatively, a change of house-type might produce savings that could be allocated to the plot, making a quick purchase more likely.

Spend time drafting a realistic budget. It'll help you to focus on how you'll finance the project, the size and type of house, how the house will be built and all the associated costs. But, most important for you at this stage, it shows you how much you can afford to spend on your plot.

CHAPTER 5 THE PRICE

Having decided what you want to build and where, how you want to set about the project, how much it's all going to cost and how you're going to fund it, you're now ready to find and buy a building plot. Buying a plot isn't like buying a house or even a car. A plot's value lies in the sort of house it can accommodate, rather than in the land itself. Understanding what determines plot prices will help you in your search.

PLANNING PERMISSIONS

A building plot is development land, the value of which is determined by its planning permission. Many plots are sold with the benefit of outline planning permission (permission in principle in Scotland) which establishes the principle that some sort of dwelling can be built on the plot. Detailed or full planning permission is for a specific size and design of house, the full details of which are all part of the permission. Both types of planning permission create development value in the plot. If a plot has planning permission for, say, a bungalow or a modest three-bedroom house, obviously, its value is going to be lower than if the permission was for a large five-bedroom house.

In practice things aren't always so simple. Existing planning permissions don't always reflect the full potential of the plot. A plot with permission for a two-bedroom house and worth £80,000 might actually be viable for a four-bedroom luxury house with a plot value of £150,000. The person who gets that additional value is the one who spots and exploits the potential. This could be the existing owner or it could be an astute purchaser who buys and then gets a new planning permission. Occasionally, a plot has planning permission for one house but is large enough for two or three - the sort of opportunity which property developers dream of. Although your prime motivation might be to build your dream home, don't ignore the possibility of stumbling on a gold mine.

A common misconception is that one can simply buy a piece of agricultural land for £2,000 or £3,000, obtain planning permission and create a building plot. If land has no planning permission but there's potential for obtaining it, this is normally reflected in the price. Where a plot lies outside a residential area, its price can be affected by its potential for other uses, for example offices next door might desperately need more floor space or extra parking. The price the owners would pay for adjoining land suitable for their purposes could be higher than its value as a building plot. Beware also 'leisure plots' or 'lots' of land sold as an investment or leisure opportunity with alleged potential for planning permission in the future. Such plots rarely have any realistic potential and might turn out to be no more than overpriced agricultural land.

EFFECTS ON VALUE

The value of a plot depends on what can be built on it, less all the costs of creating that building. A range of practical considerations can affect the cost of developing a plot and, therefore, its value - ground conditions, services, access problems - and Part Three covers all these in detail. Anything that adds unusual cost to the build, or restricts how a plot can be developed, should be reflected in the price. At the time a plot is put on the market, the vendors might be unaware of problems that could come to light and affect the eventual sale price. It's for buyers to investigate plots thoroughly.

Market conditions have a profound effect on the value of plots and, as with any commodity, supply and demand are the determining forces. The plot market is very closely linked to the fortunes of the housing market, with national fluctuations, and regional, county and local variations. These affect price levels and also supply and demand for different sectors of the market, like detached houses or terraced houses.

In a buoyant housing market, building plots become attractive to developers, builders and speculators. Plot prices rise, fuelled by demand and the prospect of house prices rising during the time taken to build the house. In these conditions, self-builders are at a disadvantage unless they enter the market fully prepared.

You might not be intending to sell your finished house for profit, but you can still lose out to builders and developers, even though they have to allow for a profit in their calculations. Builders can promise the estate agent who sells them a plot, the handling of the sale of the finished house in return. This opportunity to earn another commission gives estate agents a powerful incentive to sell to builders. Some agents automatically offer any plots they get only to a few favoured builders. Established builders can show a good track record of paying a fair price, buying quickly and being reliable. In comparison you're an unknown quantity who'll only be taken seriously if you're thoroughly prepared and give the impression that you know exactly what you're doing.

A depressed housing market is often a much more fertile environment for self-builders provided they can get obtain finance. Builders and developers are cautious, their bids for plots reflect the low or falling price they might get for the finished house and the risk that they might not be able to sell it for months or years. You've no such worries and in these conditions, can often outbid builders. There's also less time pressure - you can, for example, assess the plot thoroughly, obtain your planning permission and double-check your budget before committing to the purchase.

Good sites are always in demand, whatever the state of the market. Plots of 0.2 hectare (half-an-acre) or more in a rural or semi-rural setting, not too far from shops or station, and perhaps with a view, fetch surprisingly high prices even in the most depressed market. Similarly, plots in select small towns and villages, noted perhaps for their charm, attract much higher prices than those in less favoured towns or villages nearby.

Whatever the state of the market, never pay a price higher than your personal estimation of the value of the plot. Asking prices can be very misleading - in a busy market they're frequently exceeded, sometimes by large margins, and in a quiet market they can be hopelessly optimistic. Often no firm asking price is quoted, instead offers are invited or a guide price is given. This emphasises that it's for you to make an offer which the seller will then accept or reject.

Before you start plot-searching answer the check list (right) and use it as the basis for your search and for briefing agents on your requirements.

PRICE GUIDE

We look at how to value a plot in Part Four, but to estimate the price you'll have to pay, watch the market. Get a general idea of price levels from several estate agents who sell plots in your area of search. Try to talk to other people who've bought plots recently. You'll soon discover the level of local prices. Look at your budget again to work out a general price guide for yourself which shouldn't be within narrow bands. If you've £90,000 available for the plot, set your price guide nearer £110,000 to ensure that, when you set out to find a plot, you don't miss over-priced plots which might have been on the market for many months.

REQUIREMENTS CHECK LIST

Preferred size and type of house
Type (bungalow/chalet/house)
Number of bedrooms
Total floor area (sq m or sq ft)
Style of house

Size of plot
Minimum frontage
Area (sq m, hectares or acres)

Type and location of plot
Setting (town/village/country)
Type (individual/group/estate)

Area of search
List all towns and villages within area of search

Source of finance
Equity in existing house
Capital available
Maximum mortgage/loan
Name of bank/building society

Preliminary budget
Available finance
Estimated total building costs
Amount available for plot

Price guide for plot
Approx. minimum
Approx. maximum

PART 2 FINDING THE PLOT

Building plots for sale can be few and far between. Plots vary enormously in area, character and price and in their suitability for the size and type of house you intend building. If you want some degree of choice - or in some areas to find a plot at all - you need to investigate as many different sources as possible. Good plots sell quickly as builders and developers seek out the really prime sites. Only problem plots stay on the market for months or years. You'll probably not find a perfect plot on the market the moment you start looking. You might be lucky but more likely you'll have to use some of the plot-finding methods suggested here.

CHAPTER 6

WHERE TO LOOK

In this chapter, we look at where most plots are sold or advertised - a good place to begin your search.

ESTATE AGENTS

Most plots are sold through estate agents, except in Scotland where sales are shared equally between estate agents and solicitors. Scottish solicitors operate property centres, like large estate agents' offices, where houses and plots are sold. Unlike estate agents, property centres advertise all sites being sold by solicitors in the area. In the south of England and home counties, plots aren't usually widely advertised by agents in the same way as houses are, although in the west, midlands and north this is more normal. Not all estate agents deal with the sale of plots; of those that do, some have specialist land departments, while others sell only one or two plots a year.

If you're plot-hunting in an area you don't know, use the internet or look in Yellow Pages for the names and telephone numbers of

GWYNELLS

The Estate Agents

Offices also at: Aberfall, Llanfern, Lunffordd Cross, Maerdon and Newydd Cwmwysg

FOR SALE

RESIDENTIAL BUILDING PLOT
APPROXIMATELY 0.20 ACRES (0.083 HA)
PENGROES LANE, TAL-Y-NANTY

With Outline Planning Permission for a Detached Dwelling

Exceptional position on the Edge of this Pleasant Village

Distant Sea Views

Benefitting from Established Mature Gardens

LOCATION

The site is located on the outskirts of the village of Tal-y-Nanty adjoining Pincelli Cottage, Pengroes Lane. Tal-y-Nanty is a popular village located south west of Abberaban and benefits from a primary school, general store, public house and chapel.

DESCRIPTION

The plot has an open southerly aspect with views of the sea. It extends to 0.20 acres (0.08 ha) with a frontage of 60 ft (18 m) and a depth of about 150 ft (45 m). A former paddock, the plot is mostly laid to grass with established tees and shrubs along the northern boundary.

MISREPRESENTATION ACT/MISDESCRIPTIONS ACT

Gwynells for themselves and for the vendors or lessors of this property whose agents they are give notice that: (i) the particulars are set out as a general outline only for the guidance of intending purchasers or lessees, and do not constitute, nor constitute part of, an offer or contract; (ii) all descriptions, dimensions, references to condition and necessary permission for use and occupation and other details are given without responsibility and any intending purchasers or tenants should not reply on them as statements or representations of fact but must satisfy themselves by inspection or otherwise as to the correctness of each of them; (iii) no person in the employment of Gwynells has any authority o give any representation or warranty whatever n relation to this property

Estate agents' particulars vary in content and detail and these show information typically available – many also

PLANNING
Outline planning permission was granted at appeal dated 13th September 2009, under application reference number F/1149/09, for the erection of one dwelling.

SERVICES
All main services are understood to be available in close proximity to the site but prospective purchasers will be expected to satisfy themselves as to the availability and adequacy of these services by making their own enquiries of the appropriate service company.

TERMS
The purchaser will be responsible for erecting a 6 ft (1.8 m) close board fence along the southern boundary of the site within one month of completion of the sale or before commencement of the building works whichever is sooner.

PRICE
Offers are invited for the Freehold in the region of £125.000.

VIEWING
Strictly by appointment with Gwynells.

DIRECTIONS
From this office turn along High Street and take the third right into Oak Lane. The plot will be found 1.5 miles down the lane on the left.

Figure 6.1

include an Ordnance Survey location or site plan

local estate agents. Start with the large multi-office practices and with firms of chartered surveyors who are involved in estate agency, as these usually offer a wide range of property services. Not all large estate agents deal in plots but those that do may well have the widest selection. If these firms don't deal with plots, they should be able to point you in the right direction.

Most estate agents who regularly sell plots keep an applicants register with details of people who are looking and the type and location of plots they want. Agents generally have a form to be filled in and this information is held on a database. To be included on the register, you can telephone, call in or write to agents, but your best bet is to do all three. Some agents' websites enable you to register your interest on line. Telephone to make an appointment, go to the meeting with a clear definition of your requirements, and follow up afterwards with a letter confirming your ability to make a quick and sensible offer for the right piece of land. This helps mark you out as a serious buyer and distinguishes you from many people who turn up with only the vaguest idea of what they're looking for and how much they can afford to spend. Register with all agents who sell plots in your area of search. Any estate agent could potentially be asked to sell a plot. Concentrate your effort on the main agents but don't ignore the others altogether.

Once registered with agents, remind them of your interest regularly. You're likely to be one of many – possibly hundreds – who have registered for plots and need to get yourself to the top of the list so that, when a new site comes in, you're at the front of the queue. Be persistent but do stop short of harassment. If the agent has a steady turnover of plots and advertises regularly, ring a day or two before the advertisements are published to get ahead of any competition. Remember, estate agents owe buyers nothing as they work for, and are paid by, the vendor - the person for whom they sell the plot. The amount of help and information you get from agents can vary widely. Some are willing and able to give you information about planning permission and services (drainage, gas, water, electricity). Others give no more than brief particulars showing the location of the site often with phrases like 'it is for purchasers to satisfy themselves as to the position and availability of services', and 'all enquiries regarding planning should be addressed to the Local Planning Authority'.

Some agents send out particulars of sites which they're not directly instructed to sell which means that, if you successfully buy such a plot, the agent expects you to pay his fee, not the vendor. This should be clearly stated on the particulars along with the agents' fee or commission basis. If you're interested in the plot, contact the agent first to establish exactly what fee you'd be liable for and when, if you went ahead and bought

ESTATE AGENTS' ABBREVIATIONS USED IN PLOT ADS

PP	Planning Permission
OPP	Outline Planning Permission
DPP	Detailed Planning Permission
FPP	Full Planning Permission
F/H	Freehold
L/H	Leasehold
OIRO	Offers In the Region Of
ONO	Or Nearest Offer

Figure 6.2

the plot. In these circumstances, the agent is working for you, and might be prepared to do more work on your behalf, to earn his fee, including obtaining planning documents, checking availability and cost of service connections and negotiating the price.

Even if a particular agent doesn't routinely offer this sort of introduction service, there's nothing to stop you putting the idea to them. Put in writing that you're willing to pay them an introductory commission – on a fixed or percentage basis – if they come up with a plot that you end up purchasing. This gives them a powerful incentive to have you at the top of their list of people to contact when they hear of plots on the market being sold by other agents. When owners are thinking of selling plots they'll probably get several agents around before deciding which one to use so there'll be a few local agents who know sites are about to be sold and you can tap into this knowledge to get ahead of the crowd.

Agents' particulars are the butt of many jokes - 'good transport links to major cities' means next to a motorway; 'convenient for the airport' means at the end of the runway; 'land with potential' means a plot without planning permission. The Property Misdescriptions Act (1991) was passed to put an end to such entertaining use of language. No matter how accurate particulars appear to be, you should always check for yourself any claims made and information given and watch out for omissions (see Figs 6.1 & 6.2).

Whether or not you relish the prospect of dealing with agents, you can use the internet as well as or instead of contacting their offices, especially during the early stages of searching. Most agents put their sale properties onto websites and you can search for land and plots for sale or go to the various agents' sites to monitor what they have on their books. The internet can be very effective for this, enabling you to sift through a large number of potential sites quickly and to pick up a good deal of valuable market intelligence, such as asking prices and availability. Using websites means you can avoid receiving huge quantities of inappropriate particulars but won't put you ahead of the game or tip you off about plots that scarcely make it to the open market before being snapped up.

Figure 6.3

Particulars available on an auctioneer's website set out basic site information

AUCTIONS

Sometimes plots are sold at auctions held by local estate agents and by large property practices specialising in such sales. The latter tend to deal with sales of land owned by bankrupt businesses and by other property-owning bodies. If you register with local estate agents they should tell you about any plots they're selling at auction and keep an eye on property adverts in the local newspapers as well. You can find out about national and regional auctions by searching the internet which can tell you whether plots are to be sold in your target area. Auctioneers' websites allow you to see basic information about the lots for sale and give details of the auction. Otherwise, auctions are advertised in specialist property magazines - Estates Gazette and Property Week. An example of auction particulars is given in Figure 6.3.

PROPERTY PROFESSIONALS

Surveyors, building surveyors, architects, architectural technicians and planning consultants might know of plots coming up for sale, either through their contacts in the property business, or through their work on specific sites. A telephone call to them could produce details of an ideal plot which is to be sold when planning permission is granted. This is likely to work best where you have some kind of relationship with such professionals or would be prepared to use their services as they would then have a vested interest in helping you. Advance notice of such sites puts you well ahead of the competition and might even mean you can buy before the plot ever comes onto the market.

LOCAL NETWORK

Use the local grapevine - family, friends, neighbours, colleagues and other contacts - to help you find a plot. You've only got one pair of eyes and ears and a limited amount of time to devote to land finding but by enlisting all your contacts you can multiply this tens of times over. Make sure everyone knows you're in the market to buy a building plot. They might know of someone with land for sale or with land that could make a suitable plot, or spot an advert or agents' board you've missed. Put up notices at your place of work, social clubs, pubs, church and anywhere else you can think of, saying that you're looking for a plot to build a house on. You can increase your chances of success dramatically by offering a reward for information that leads to the successful purchase of a site, perhaps £1,000. This might sound a lot but it's likely to be less than 1 per cent of your total cost and could easily make the difference between being able to build your own home or not.

LOCAL NEWSPAPERS

These are essential reading as they contain a wealth of useful information. Plots are advertised by estate agents or private individuals, listed under 'Houses for Sale', 'Land', 'Building Land' or 'Building Plots'. Local papers also have pages of houses for sale which give you an instant impression of the local housing market – what's available, price levels and which agents are active in particular areas. Scan the advertisements carefully, as plots can be hidden away among other properties, for example, 'Delightful Four bed Victorian house, living room, dining room, kitchen, garage, large orchard/ possible building plot'. Some local papers list all local planning applications and Chapter 7 explains how to use this information.

Consider placing your own advertisement in a local paper saying 'building plot wanted', stating whether you want a plot for a house or bungalow, and the area, and giving your telephone number. This could root out plots that might not otherwise come to light, including ones owned by builders or vendors who, for various reasons, might not want to publicise their land for sale widely. It could, on the other hand, produce a clutch of complete no-hopers that owners haven't been able to shift elsewhere – you won't know unless you try.

MAGAZINES

Look at specialist magazines catering for self-builders, particularly Build It, Homebuilding and Renovating and Self-build and Design, which advertise plots and conversion opportunities for sale (see Figure 6.4). Most properties listed are on the market through estate agents but some sellers, wishing to avoid agents' fees, only advertise their properties there. As well as the possibility of finding your plot in the listings, you can also see how many plots come up in your area, the level of asking prices and which agents are active in that area. Plots are also advertised in

Plots and conversion and renovation properties are listed in several self-build mags

papers like Exchange and Mart and Daltons Weekly, which also have searchable websites, and in the property pages of some national newspapers.

SELF-BUILD PACKAGE COMPANIES

Self-build package companies give varying degrees of help with land finding. If you're going to buy a house package from a particular company, obviously it'll be anxious to help you in your plot-search, as much as it can but bear in mind that, understandably, most companies are really interested in people who already have a site. Some have lists of building plots and/or names of agents and consultants who sell or find plots. Others give more active help and advice on plot buying. If you plan to buy a package, try speaking to a few companies and see what they can do for you.

BUILDERS MERCHANTS

The larger chains of builders merchants are increasingly geared up to help self-builders and this includes efforts to help their potential customers find land and, thereby, turn them into actual customers. Some maintain a register of plots on the market in their area, partly drawing on their contacts with local builders and tradesmen. Find out if the builders merchants in your area keep a plot list or what other help is available. A local builders merchant would also be a good place to leave a 'plot wanted' advertisement as local builders and trades people see a lot of properties and have their ears to the ground.

SHOWS AND EXHIBITIONS

Major self-build shows are held each year in Birmingham, London and Swindon, and smaller regional shows are held throughout the country and these are advertised in the self-build magazines. Plot finding services, self-build package companies and other useful organisations are represented at the shows. A chat with staff on the stands gives you an idea of what services they provide, about plot availability and the land market, and could provide you with some leads to follow up.

BUILDERS AND DEVELOPERS

Builders and developers sometimes own plots which they're prepared to sell, rather than build on themselves. Housing developers sometimes sell off individual plots in a larger scheme (see Figure 6.5) although, to protect their own interests and depending on the circumstances, they might want to vet the design of the house to be built. Other developers cater specifically for self-builders: obtaining planning permission; sub-dividing the site; putting in access roads and services; and then selling individual plots.

From your local research you might be aware of plots owned by builders where work doesn't seem to be starting or you might spot a development where part of the site has been left unbuilt. Where you see this, get in contact with the builder or developer concerned to find out whether they would consider selling to you. Otherwise, a circular letter sent to local builders (addresses in Yellow Pages or on Yell.com) might produce results. Be precise and brief in your letter. For example:

'I am a cash buyer actively looking for a building plot in the Buckbridge/ Wingley area, and am ready to go ahead now. The plot must be suitable for a two-storey, four-

Figure 6.5

Builders and developers building estates of houses are sometimes prepared to sell off plots to individuals so look out for sites under construction, especially where some plots seem to be left undeveloped

bedroom house of about 1,700 square feet, 170 square metres. If you have, or know of any suitable plots in the area, please telephone me on 123456 daytimes or 7891011 evenings.'

In places where estate agents only sell plots to a few local builders, you're effectively excluded from buying. If you come across this, and intend to use a builder to build your house anyway, say in your letter that you would retain the builder to do the work. This gives the builder extra incentive to sell to you, but you must find out about the cost and quality of their work before you commit yourself.

COUNCILS

Most county and district/borough councils (and their equivalents in Scotland and Wales) own land in their areas, some of which can be suitable for building single houses or for conversion. Telephone their estates departments or visit the council's website to find out what's available. This varies between councils: where building land is scarce, there might be nothing but you never know; elsewhere, councils are keen to help and sometimes sell serviced plots specifically for self-builders or assist self-build groups. If you're interested in joining a self-build group, the council might be able to tell you about any that are forming locally. If you have modest means and are interested in a community self-build project, try contacting the charity Community Self Build Agency. The Homes and Communities Agency sells land, through its agents, including single plots to individuals.

MAJOR LANDOWNERS

Large landowning bodies, like railway companies, the electricity, gas and water companies, breweries and BT plc, sometimes sell surplus land suitable for house-building. Get the addresses of the estates departments from their websites, local offices or phone book and write or telephone with details of what you're looking for. Such organisations could well sell through estate agents or auctions but you might, nevertheless, be able to get an early indication that a property is coming up.

PLOT FINDING SERVICES

You might not have sufficient time available to search for plots yourself or you might have tried and failed to find the right piece of land - if so, consider getting help. There's a range of services available from plot listing companies, estate agents and some other specialist companies. Look for these services in the self-build magazines or search on line to see what is available.

If you're considering paying for help, there's a golden rule: get written confirmation of precisely what's going to be done, for how long, at what cost, and the circumstances in which you become liable for a fee or commission. Payment for plot-finding is often based on a commission - a percentage of the purchase price - paid either at exchange of contracts or completion. The percentage must be agreed at the outset and you should check whether out-of-pocket expenses are included. Alternatively, a fixed fee might be charged for the plot search or a fee based on the time taken. Beware of arrangements that seem open ended. You might be asked to pay a 'retainer' in advance of any work being done. Make sure you know whether this is refunded if no plot is found, or if it's deducted from the final fee or commission if you buy a plot. Land finding services come and go and you need to be careful, especially with internet based ones.

SEARCH RESULTS

Searching for self-build plots in Cumbershire

LOCATION	DETAILS
Ballistick REF 8457	A small plot with planning permission for a detached four bedroomed house in a residential area. Guide Price £99,995.
Ballistick REF 8078	A site with planning permission for a pair of four bedroomed detached houses in a sought-after village. Guide Price £400,000
Dassle REF 7776	A plot of approx. 0.18 acres with planning permission for a detached four bedroomed house in a residential village setting. Guide Price £295,000.
Dassle REF 7212	A plot with planning permission for a detached six bedroomed house in a prime village setting. OIEO £600,000.
Dassle REF 8013	A plot with planning permission for the erection of a two/three bedroomed detached bungalow. Guide Price £205,000.
Limber REF 7567	A plot of approx. 0.5 acres with planning permission for a detached four bedroomed chalet house on a semi rural main road. Guide Price £285,000.
Niggle End REF 8976	A plot with outline planning permission for one house. OIEO £125,000.
Niggle End REF 7920	A plot with outline planning permission for the erection of a single detached chalet bungalow and double garage. OIRO £150,000.
Stemple Cross REF 8050	A plot with planning permission for a replacement four bedroomed detached house in the town. Guide Price £225,000- £250,000.

Figure 6.6

Search results from an internet plot-finding website giving brief details and asking price

Some services simply identify likely plots leaving you to do the rest, while others are more comprehensive, taking you through to completing the purchase. There are self-build packages that provide plot-finding as part of a service including site assessment, valuation, planning permission, purchase, Building Regulations and project management. Estate agents who sell land sometimes look for plots for clients as well; the sort of arrangement depends entirely on what you agree with them. Usually there's no fee unless you buy a plot that the agent finds for you, in which case you pay a commission or finder's fee of 1 or 2 per cent.

There are specialist companies offering computerised database plot-finding services specifically for self-builders, well established ones include Plotbrowser, Plotfinder and Plotsearch. With some you subscribe to obtain access to all the details on the database, with others access is free. This type of service is especially useful if you're searching for a plot a long way from your existing home but, because the land market often moves quickly, entries can be out of date and the lists can include plots that agents are having trouble selling. On the other hand, some sites go only to land-finding agencies and so are only available to their subscribers. Apart from finding a plot directly, the computerised listings provide valuable market information - the areas in which plots are coming up, the level of asking prices and who handles the sale of plots in your area of search (see Figure 6.6). Such market information alone is usually well worth the subscription.

With any type of plot-finding service, read the small print carefully as with some you can be liable to pay another fee, if you buy a plot through the agency. Make sure you understand what sort of information or service you're going to be given.

CHAPTER 7

HIDDEN OPPORTUNITIES

So far we've looked at finding building plots being offered for sale. Professional property developers, though, don't wait for sites to come onto the market. They seek out land with planning permission that hasn't been developed or look for suitable sites, see whether they can get planning permission and whether the owner will sell - there's nothing to stop you using the same methods.

PLANNING RECORDS

As building plots need planning permission, a good place to look is in the planning records. District, borough and city councils, or in metropolitan and a few other areas, unitary councils, deal with day-to-day planning matters in England. In Scotland they're dealt with by the councils, in Wales by county or county borough councils and in Northern Ireland by the divisional offices of the Planning Service. For convenience we'll use the term 'district council' throughout this book to cover all of these. District councils keep records in their planning departments of all past and present planning applications, which are available for public inspection. You can find out if a particular piece of land has planning permission or if an application has been refused in the past. You should look for plots with planning permission that have not been built on, which you hope the owner will be willing to sell.

Most councils have their planning records available in some form on their websites. Many sites have comprehensive records going back several years or even decades, including plans and other documents associated with applications. Some only have recent applications or don't include any documents. The degree to which these records are searchable varies but, as a general rule, both quality and searchability are improving. Where on-line records are incomplete or inaccessible, you can call in at the council's planning department and look at the records there.

The first step is to check the records for what planning permissions exist. District councils' record systems vary, as does their enthusiasm for delving into them. Always check whether the council needs advance warning if you're going to call in as some don't produce records on demand if you just turn up but require a day or two to dig out the files. Looking up planning records can occupy an enjoyable ten minutes or several frustrating hours. Councils have microfiche records, computerised scanned records, paper files or a combination of these. Since searching through the records of a whole area would take a long time, concentrate on one town or parish at a time. An actual address or, better still, a planning application reference number, speeds things up but you don't need to know who owns the site in order to look up the records. There's a record of every planning permission, often listed by parish or other area. Go back over these and make a note of all permissions for houses, including the name and address of the person who made the application. Some district councils also mark the reference number of all planning applications on Ordnance Survey maps, making it easy to see where applications have been made, but not what the applications were actually for. Study the maps to identify likely sites where an application has been made and write down the reference number and address. Look up the application or ask for the planning record card of the property, which sets out its history of applications.

Some permissions won't be for the right type of house, or in the right place; others, you might know, have already been built. Any remaining sites should be checked by a visit to see if work has started.

District councils produce a list of the planning applications made each week which you can see on their website, at their offices, at parish council offices, local libraries or listed in a local newspaper. This list gives the reference, type of application and address, for example, 'R/98/1648, outline, single detached dwelling and double garage, Mill Lane, Riverton'. You can ask at the planning department to see the application which contains useful information, including the size and location of the plot, and who owns it.

An application made in outline is generally a better bet than a detailed application, as outline is often used to establish the principle that a house can be built on the plot before it's sold. A detailed application can mean that the scheme is farther advanced and that either the owner is going to build or has a buyer already. In some situations, for example, in Conservation Areas, district councils are likely to require all applications to be made in detail. So, if an application alerts you to a suitable plot, pursue it regardless of the type of application involved.

LOCAL PLANS AND LOCAL DEVELOPMENT FRAMEWORKS

District councils draw up documents containing planning policies for their area. The system is currently changing and whilst the old Local Plan-based approach used to be somewhat complex, sadly the new system is even more complicated and ridden with bewildering jargon and initials. Planning policies are now to be set out in Local Development Frameworks (LDFs) in England, Local Development Plans (LDPs) in Scotland and Wales, and in Development Plans in Northern Ireland. We'll use the initials LDF to cover all these plans. Not all councils have completed the changeover from Local Plans to LDFs so you must check on the council's website which applies and, if in doubt, ring up and ask a council planning policy officer.

Planning policy documents consist of a written part, setting out the district council's development policies, and a proposals map. Local Plans contained all the policies in one document; LDFs comprise a number of documents. The written parts of these documents distinguish the actual planning policies from

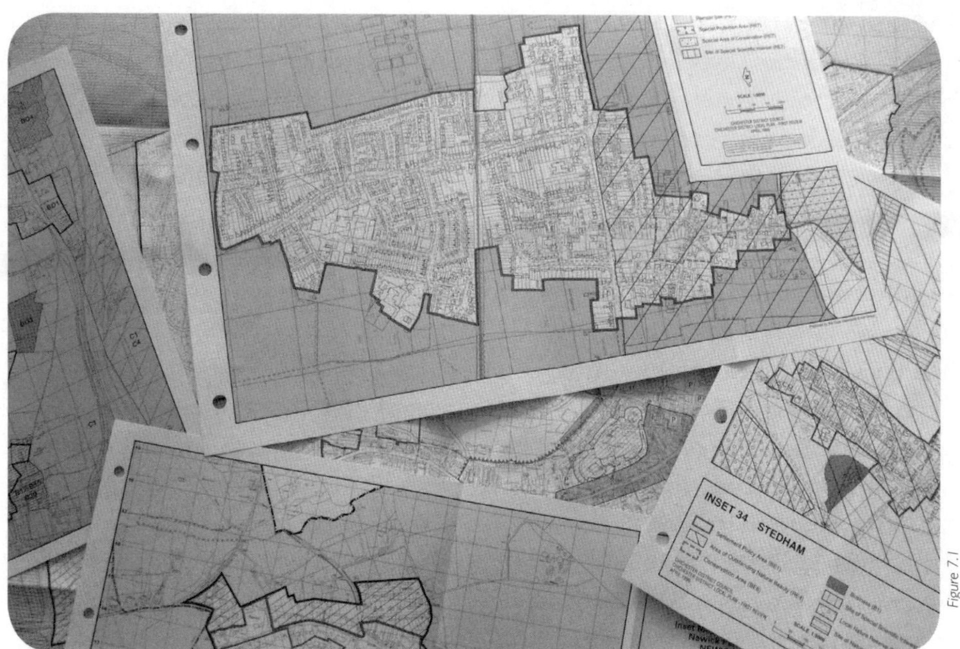

Figure 7.1

Local Development Framework and Local Plan inset maps are detailed and mostly up to date, which you can use to identify land allocated for housing and the areas within the settlement boundary where planning permission is likely to be given

the accompanying explanation and justification. A proposals map shows the area covered by the document, indicating where various policies apply and identifying individual sites for development. Selected areas are shown in greater detail on inset maps, where this is necessary to make the policies clear (see Figure 7.1).

Local Plans are sometimes confused with Structure Plans, formerly prepared by county councils or groups of councils, which set out more general planning policies for a county or sub-region. Often people involved with property use terms such as 'local structure plan' or 'village development plan' which are technically meaningless (but can be useful nevertheless as they betray the users' fragile understanding of the subtleties of the planning system).

Under the old system, a slightly different type of plan was used in Wales, in metropolitan areas (Greater London, Greater Manchester, Merseyside, South Yorkshire, Tyne and Wear, West Midlands and West

Yorkshire) and by just a few other English councils. Here Structure and Local Plans were combined into one document called a Unitary Development Plan and, like old-style Local Plans, you might still come across this type of plan as some have yet to be replaced.

Local Plans and LDFs usually distinguish between 'settlements' and 'countryside'. Settlements are towns, villages and, perhaps, small hamlets. Around each settlement a line is drawn on the proposals map (see Figure 7.1), which is known variously as the 'Settlement Boundary', 'Built Up Area Boundary', 'Housing Framework' or 'Village Envelope' but all terms mean the same. Beyond this line, restrictive policies apply, which mean that opportunities for building on greenfield sites in the countryside are very few and far between. On the other hand, policies inside settlement boundaries generally allow new houses to be built in residential areas and sites for new housing estates are shown. Example planning policies are given in Figure 7.2. Settlement boundaries don't always follow obvious lines - the outskirts of towns and villages can be excluded and so be considered 'countryside' in planning terms.

Local Plans and LDFs show Conservation Areas, Green Belts, Areas of Outstanding Natural Beauty (AONB), or National Scenic Areas in Scotland, and other specially designated areas. All these designations restrict to some extent the type and nature of development that can take place within their boundaries.

Look at the Local Plan or LDF covering your area of search at the district council's offices or at a local library. Study the proposals map to identify likely sites or areas where there might be plots. You can then research the planning history of the site or area, in the way described in the previous section, to find out if planning permission has been granted and who owns the land. Use the Local Plan or LDF if you find a potential plot without planning permission; look it up on the proposals map to see whether it comes in an area where development is allowed. The companion to this book, How to Get Planning Permission, has more detail on planning applications, appeals and Local Plans/LDFs.

ORDNANCE SURVEY MAPS

If you're determined to build in one particular area, say a small village or neighbourhood in a town, obtain the Ordnance Survey map or maps

LOCAL PLAN POLICIES

Local Development Framework/Local Plan policy for new housing in the countryside

New dwellings in the countryside and in settlements without Village Policy Boundaries will not be permitted unless justified in connection with the essential needs of agriculture or forestry subject to the criteria laid down in Policy AG4.

Local Development Framework/Local Plan policy for new housing in settlements

Within the defined settlement boundaries, planning permission will normally be granted for proposals for residential development, only if the following criteria are met:

1 The land is not allocated for some other purpose in this plan
2 The character and form respect that of the general locality
3 Efficient use is made of the land in terms of density and as general guidance residential development should be provided at average net densities of at least 30 dwellings per hectare
4 The provision of car parking and vehicle manoeuvring do not significantly reduce garden areas or adversely affect adjoining property
5 The adjoining highways have the capacity to accommodate the additional traffic generated by the development
6 Other normal development control criteria can be met

Figure 7.2

Planning polices, which govern where and what you can build, are set out in the council's Local Development Framework or Local Plan

that cover it. Ordnance Survey maps at 1:2,500 or 1:1,250 scale show individual houses, gardens and pieces of land, enabling you to identify potential plots. Figure 7.3 shows the amount of detail the maps give. You're limited in what you can see on the ground by boundary walls and hedges, trees and bushes within sites and existing buildings. Ordnance Survey maps allow you to see the gaps and spaces between buildings without such obstacles. You can buy the maps on-ine or from local Ordnance Survey agents, whose addresses are in Yellow Pages or

ORDNANCE SURVEY MAPS

Figure 7.3

Use Ordnance Survey maps to spot possible plots – rear gardens, side gardens, vacant sites - bearing in mind where planning policy boundaries lie, which you can mark on the map as well as the potential plots you identify

Yell.com, but each map only covers a relatively small area and they're expensive. Libraries also keep copies of local Ordnance Survey maps. Check the date of the map, in some areas even the most up-to-date are over ten years old and much could have changed in that time.

AERIAL IMAGES

Google Earth, Google Maps and other similar on-line resources enable you to view areas of land in some detail. Unlike Ordnance Survey maps, boundaries can be hard to pick out and the full extent of sites obscured, especially where there are trees, but they do provide a wealth of information none-the-less. You can get a good feel for what's on and around potential plots and the general pattern of development in the vicinity. Google's 'street view' facility adds a further level of sophistication to the process, which is helpful if you're looking in an area remote from where you live.

IDENTIFYING POTENTIAL PLOTS ON THE GROUND

Local Plans/LDF maps, Ordnance Survey maps and aerial images might help identify likely places to find plots but you should also explore your area of search by car, bicycle or on foot. It's worth spending time in the area anyway, especially if you're not already living there, as you never know what you might come across while you're looking for new plot opportunities, such as a plot with a 'for sale' board of an agent with whom you've not registered. Look for things like gaps in an otherwise built-up road frontage, houses with large gardens that could be sub-divided, and extra long or extra wide plots. Figure 7.4 gives an idea of the opportunities. Don't confine your search to existing residential property. Commercial property, like workshops, lock-up sheds, shops, disused accesses, closed down pubs, utility buildings and land, offices, and car parks, can equally make perfectly suitable plots or conversion properties. Plots can be created by combining land in two or more different ownerships, for example adjoining side gardens, neither of which would be large enough on their own, could be amalgamated to create a site wide enough to build on. Don't be unduly swayed by what's on the land at the moment; trees, hedges, overgrown shrubs, weeds and brambles, sheds and garages can obscure potential plots, so you need to use your imagination. Look for any adequately-sized pieces of land,

IDENTIFYING POTENTIAL PLOTS

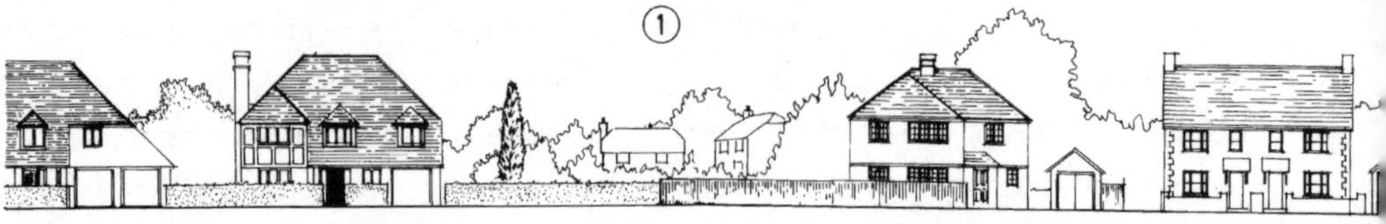

Look in your chosen area of search for opportunities to create plots such as (1) combining

especially frontages, and picture what could fit on it, if existing buildings and foliage were cleared. Check whether it's possible for access from the plot to the road to be arranged. Envisage where a house could be sited on the plot and whether this would fit in with the surroundings or would affect the privacy of neighbouring houses. If there might be problems of this kind, see whether they could be overcome by siting the house in a different place, by a clever design or by landscaping. These preliminary questions determine whether you've found a possible plot worth investigating further.

A word here about so called 'backland' and 'tandem' development. This is where a large back garden is sub-divided to create a plot, often with an access drive running past the existing house and down the side of its garden to the plot. Backland development isn't satisfactory where existing properties would lose their privacy or where there would be noise and disturbance from the use of a new drive. Government planning policies encourage more intensive use of land in towns and villages and it's often possible for houses on backland plots to be designed so that these problems don't occur. Some district councils' seem to oppose backland development as a matter of principle, almost regardless of the merits of the case, and so applications are turned down which might be granted planning permission at appeal. In some areas, backland development is an established part of the local pattern of building, so don't dismiss these sites. They can make ideal plots, especially if you're looking for a quiet spot away from a road.

THE PLOT IN YOUR GARDEN

Many people who build their own houses do so in the garden of their existing home - don't overlook the

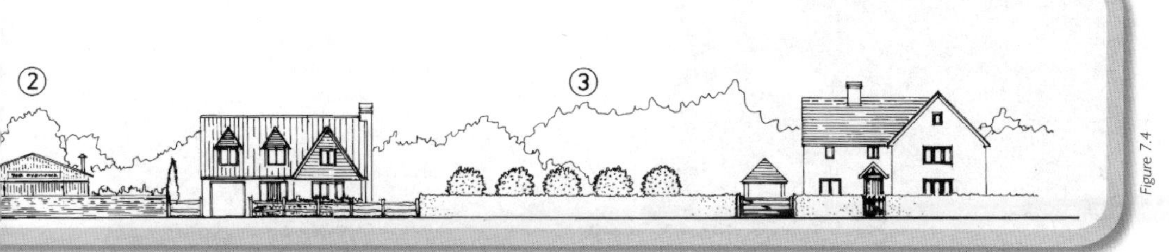

side gardens, (2) demolishing buildings, (3) orchards, paddocks, tennis courts or large gardens

possibilities there might be on your doorstep (see Figure 7.5). If there's not enough space, think about buying-in adjoining land to make a plot. Beyond this, look for houses on the market that have a plot, or potential plot, in the garden. You can buy the house and either sell it straight away, just keeping the plot, or live in it while you build, and then sell. There could be some sobering cash-flow implications in such an arrangement, however, there are advantages to building in your own garden. Your new home design is less likely to be limited by covenants; access, drainage and fencing can be easier to arrange; and you can live on the site to supervise and monitor the build in comfort. There's plenty of scope to profit from creating your own plot but profit is closely linked to risk. If you buy a house and plot with planning permission, you'll probably pay the full market price for both. If you buy a house with a large garden with potential, you'll run the risk of being refused planning permission.

DEMOLITION AND REBUILD

Existing houses and other buildings can provide opportunities for demolition and rebuilding (see Figures 7.6 and 7.7). Where the existing house is sub-standard, small or just doesn't make the most of a site, the economics of replacement often stack up better but there's actually nothing to stop most houses being pulled down and new ones being built in their place. In countryside areas this might be the only way to get planning permission for new houses. In such areas, when looking at sub-standard or long unoccupied houses, you need to ensure that they haven't lost their residential use rights. This can arise where a house is so dilapidated that it isn't capable of being occupied or where it's been used for some other purpose. Local planning policies on replacement houses, and how they're

Figure 7.5

Some lucky people have a potential plot in their own garden, although planning policies, access, ground conditions and covenants still have to be checked – in some areas, building in rear gardens is discouraged

interpreted, vary between district councils, therefore, ask a planning officer how applications for demolition and rebuild are dealt with locally.

Remember, planning policies are likely to be different for settlements and countryside. Policies often limit the size of replacement houses in the countryside, particularly in Green Belt, although, through clever design, you might be able to come up with a building which looks less conspicuous than the original but which is actually larger. If the buildings to be replaced are a pair of semi-detached houses, there's more scope for justifying an increased floor area - the reduced activity generated by one dwelling, as opposed to two, can be offset against the increase in size of building.

There are often cost savings with demolition and re-building where the existing access, services and/ or service connections, landscaping or salvageable building materials can sometimes be used.

CONVERSIONS

Many buildings lend themselves to conversion into houses, maisonettes or flats - barns, stables, schools, churches, workshops, shops, offices - even water towers and public loos have been converted (see Figures

Figure 7.6

While searching for land to build on, don't overlook the possibility of demolishing small and/or sub-standard houses as replacement is one of the few opportunities for new build in the countryside

7.8 and 7.9). Much of the guidance in this book applies equally to finding and buying conversion properties. Most properties for conversion are sold by estate agents but also look for new opportunities by travelling around the area. Bear in mind that, depending on the quality, structural stability and layout of the existing building, conversion can cost more or less than starting with a clear site.

Converting barns and rural buildings gives scope for creating new homes in the countryside although government planning guidelines say that the appearance and character of rural buildings are usually better preserved and economic activity generated by conversion to commercial, industrial or recreational uses, rather than houses. Local policies vary, but generally speaking it's easier to get planning permission to convert a rural building in a village or hamlet than for one that is isolated or on a farm. In towns and villages council policies sometimes protect certain uses from changes of use to residential, such as village shops or properties which provide employment. Check local policies to help guide you before spending too much time on searching for

Figure 7.7

Demolition and replacement of a poor quality house in an established residential area, which doesn't make the most of its site, can be a financially viable option

conversion properties.

FINDING THE OWNER

Once you've located a potential plot, you need to find the owner. Of course, if you're out and about plot-hunting you could simply ask at the nearest house or in the local pub, shop or post office. If the plot has a planning history, you can get details of the ownership at the time the applications were made from previous planning applications at the district council's offices or website. Old rating records at the council's offices might also help. If you have an address, try getting the name of the occupier from the electoral roll at a local library. The occupier is likely to own the property but could instead be a tenant who can give you the owner's name. If it's not obvious which property the potential plot belongs to, get the names of a few neighbours from the electoral roll and write or telephone to find out if they know who owns it.

You can find out who owns a property from the Land Registry, where the ownership, or title, has been registered - registration is now compulsory whenever properties change hands – however, land that's been in the same ownership for many years might well not have been registered. If the land is registered, you can get an extract from the register with information on

Figure 7.8

Existing buildings, including those on farms, offer scope for creating individual homes with plenty of character, often in places where planning permission for new houses wouldn't be given

ownership and restrictions, such as restrictive covenants, mortgages, leases or rights of way, and a title plan, which is an Ordnance Survey map marked with the boundaries of the registered title. The easiest way to do this is on-line at the Land Registry website where you can buy an extract from the register and a title plan for a small sum and download them instantly. Alternatively you can get information by post or by calling-in to inspect the register. If calling-in, it's worth telephoning first and giving the address of the property you want to look up, as this avoids having to wait while the documents are found when you arrive. When writing, you must give an address or identify the property on an Ordnance Survey map and you also need to enclose a cheque - telephone to find out current fees. The ownership information should be sent back to you within about four days. The Land Registry is a user-friendly organisation, so if you're uncertain about how to use the service, give the staff a call. Your nearest Land Registry office doesn't necessarily deal with your area; for example, the office covering Surrey is in Durham. For more information contact HM Land Registry, 32 Lincoln's Inn Fields, London WC2A 3PH (0207 9178888).

When you have the name and

Figure 7.9

In built-up areas, planning policies put fewer restrictions on conversions and a wide range of properties, like this former workshop and storage building, can make interesting homes

address, contact the owner by letter or, maybe, by a phone call or face-to-face approach, if you feel that's appropriate in the circumstances. What you say depends partly on how you've found the plot - through a new planning application, an existing permission, or by spotting an opportunity. There's no right or wrong way to make your approach but be sensitive to the fact that your contact could come out of the blue or the person might have been approached many times before. Simply say you're interested in buying the land and ask whether the owner intends to sell or would be prepared to consider or discuss the possibility. If you're lucky, the owner might be willing to sell to you and, where there's no planning permission, it's sensible to protect yourself via an appropriate legally binding contract (see Chapter 17). If the plot's already on its way to being sold, you'll at worst be ahead of the competition, at best the vendor might dispense with the time and cost of marketing through an agent and sell direct to you.

AGRICULTURAL DWELLINGS

In very limited circumstances it's possible to build a new farmhouse or an agricultural or other essential rural business worker's cottage in the countryside, where an existing agricultural business needs someone on site day and night and there's no alternative accommodation nearby. This doesn't mean you can buy an acre of agricultural land and a few chickens, call it a farm and get planning permission to build a house. District councils, backed by government advice, apply stringent tests to all such applications. Even in genuine cases of agricultural need, councils often only give a temporary planning permission for a mobile home, which has to be renewed, or upgraded to permission for a permanent house after two or three years when the need has been established beyond all reasonable doubt. These houses are subject to an 'agricultural tie', limiting who can occupy the house, and we look at this in more detail in Chapter 12. If you think you have a case to justify an agricultural dwelling, get specialist professional advice from a planning consultant.

COUNTRY HOUSES

Government planning policy advice on building in the countryside says that isolated houses of outstanding architectural merit might occasionally be allowed as an exception to the normal policies preventing new housing in rural areas. The guidance on this has changed over the years, with the emphasis shifting away from maintaining the country house tradition, to encouraging a more contemporary and cutting edge approach to design. Only a handful of such permissions are granted each year, with the majority of even well conceived schemes failing. This is a high risk, high cost route to gaining a new home and, if you contemplate it, take advice early on from a planning consultant or building designer who has knowledge or experience of it.

FINDING YOUR PLOT CHECKLIST

- Register with local estate agents
- Search agents' websites
- Read classified adverts in local papers
- Find out about plot-finding services
- Ask your building designer, self-build package company or builder for help and information on plots
- Check whether councils in the area sell single plots
- Write to local builders and housing developers
- Look at councils' planning records
- Study maps of the area
- Spend time in your area of search looking for potential plots and write to owners

PART 3

ASSESSING YOUR PLOT

Once you find what looks like the right plot, you have to be sure you can build the home you want on it. There are factors which can stop you doing this - some could rule out building altogether, others could dictate every detail of what and where you can build. You can check most aspects of your plot quite easily but some points aren't obvious and others need much investigation. To avoid costly mistakes, you must discover anything that might inhibit or add cost to the building of your house, before you agree a price or commit yourself to buying the plot. In this Part, we show you step-by-step how to assess your plot, point out pitfalls you might encounter and tell you ways to overcome them.

CHAPTER 8
FIRST CONSIDERATIONS

The first points to consider are the physical features of a plot; most of these can be assessed by looking at the site but there are those that need investigation.

FITTING THE HOUSE ON THE PLOT

Check that the home you want to build will actually fit on the plot, taking account of restrictions and neighbouring houses. With rectangular plots, it's usually a simple matter of whether the frontage is adequate for the width of the house and garage. Where a plot's an irregular shape, get a scale plan, which can be an Ordnance Survey extract taken from agents' particulars or a planning permission and enlarged on a photocopier but do ensure it's still to scale. Draw and cut out outlines of the ground-floor plan of the house and garage to the same scale, and move them around the site plan to find the best layout. If you have trouble fitting them on the plot try 'handing' the house, that is making it a mirror image of the original layout by turning your cut-out floor plan over and placing it face down. This can sometimes help solve the problem of overlooking other houses or gardens next to the plot or make the most of sunlight in main rooms of the house. Where space is limited, take check measurements on site, as site plan measurements given on application drawings and agents' particulars are often inaccurate. An error of only one metre in the plot frontage could mean that your dream home simply won't fit on the plot.

THE LIE OF THE LAND

Look at the lie of the land within the plot and in relation to the land around. Steep slopes add to build costs of the house, drive and landscaping. Earth-moving and levelling is expensive and can spoil natural contours, possibly jeopardising planning permission. If the plot is low-lying, consider the risk of flooding and whether floors would have to be set at a high level, again increasing building cost. If the plot's on high ground or in an exposed position, consider the prevailing wind and the access - a plot on a steep hill could become inaccessible in snow or icy weather. Find out if a site survey, showing levels, has been done. For plots with a steep slope you'll need a survey at some point to make sure that the scheme works. A site survey is also useful to pinpoint trees, vegetation and boundaries and in making planning and Building Regulations applications. Use your building designer to carry out a survey for you, or contact a land surveyor; you'll find these via the internet at sites like Yell.com or in Yellow Pages under 'Surveyors - Land'.

GROUND CONDITIONS

Wet or unstable ground could increase the cost of foundations. When inspecting a site in dry weather, check for areas which might be wet in winter by looking at the plant life. Clumps of reeds or rushes and willow or alder trees indicate wet ground, or possibly a spring. A line of willow or alder across a site can mark the course of an underground stream. Some areas are prone to subsidence because of mining or geological faults; look for signs like cracks, sunken areas and holes. Examples of what to look for are given in Figures 8.1, 8.2 and 8.3. Some sites comprise made-up ground, such as old clay pits or village ponds which have been filled over the years. Former industrial

CONSTRAINTS TO BUILDING

Figure 8.1

Many factors can constrain where and how you build on a plot, including the position and outlook of nearby houses, overhead cables, sewers (indicated by manhole covers), footpaths, wet ground, past landfill and trees

land might be contaminated, for example, old gas-holder sites, petrol stations, scrapyards or chemical works. Contaminated ground can be dangerous and cleaning-up costs high and, if you come across this, consider commissioning an investigation and report by a specialist consultant. Where you suspect a previous use could affect your build, look at old maps in the local library to find out about past uses of the land.

The type of soil influences the design and cost of foundations. Heavy clay and soft sand are common soil types that necessitate careful choice of foundations. Foundations can be designed to cope with poor ground conditions and in some cases the ground itself can be consolidated prior to building. The cost of special foundations might be only marginally higher than

Figure 8.2

Careful inspection of a plot should reveal most constraints to building which you should investigate, such as trees which might be protected, the possible presence of protected species, like bats or lizards, or wet ground indicating a high water table, raising potential drainage issues

standard foundations but, if your budget is very tight, poor ground conditions could mean having to look for a different plot. Speak to an officer of the building control section at the district council who can give you an idea of all likely ground condition problems found in the area. It's worth getting ground conditions checked in all cases, especially if you find anything to cause concern, so have a site investigation carried out by a builder, building surveyor or soil engineer. Ask your building designer who to use or look up 'Site Investigations' on the web or phone book.

TREES AND VEGETATION

Trees and other vegetation, like shrubs, bushes and hedges, can both help and hinder your development of a plot and so must be taken into account at an early stage. Trees are often a constraint when positioning a house on a plot, as building is usually not allowed within what's known as the 'root protection area' of the tree. You can make a rough calculation of a tree's circular root protection area by multiplying the diameter of the tree, measured at 1.5 metres from the ground, by 12, which gives you the radius of the protection area. If there's no planning permission on a plot with trees, you'll probably have to get a tree survey – or 'arboricultural impact assessment' - done, which will deal with the issue of root protection areas. District councils generally expect you to keep as many trees as possible, especially individual specimen trees and attractive groups, and can make Tree Preservation Orders, which we look at in Chapter 12.

Trees can affect the foundations of buildings, especially on shrinkable clay, where their roots dry out the soil, causing shrinkage and possibly subsidence. If trees are felled, the soil can swell subsequently, known as 'heave'. Trees with the highest water demand are elm, oak, poplar and willow.

Trees and shrubs benefit plots by providing an instant mature setting, creating privacy between neighbours and acting as a windbreak, all of which can add to the value of your finished home. They can, however, cut out light or block views. Mark on a plan the position, spread of the branches, and species of all trees on and next to the plot, and any recently cut down. If you commission a site survey, ask for these details to be included, as an accurate site survey should reduce the cost of a tree survey, should you require one. For planning purposes a tree survey must be done to a specific standard (B.S.5837:2005) and you'll need to get a suitably qualified arboriculturist to do it. A tree survey is important when working out how your house would fit onto the plot or getting foundations designed, and must be included, if you need to make a planning application.

OBSTACLES

Obstacles like telegraph poles, manhole covers or wellshafts can affect site layout and cost of the build. Manhole covers might indicate the existence of a main sewer and you can't generally build within 3 m (10 ft) of such a sewer but this sometimes varies according to its size and depth. Sewers can be diverted, assuming that an adequate gradient can be maintained, and how much this will cost depends on the distance, size and depth of sewer and the number of new manholes needed. If you can't avoid building over the line of a sewer, get quotes for the cost of having it moved. Telegraph poles and electricity supply lines can be subject to rights (or easements) which allow the service company onto the site for maintenance purposes. If there are any service supply pipes, cables or apparatus on the plot, ask your solicitor to check carefully for rights applying to them. You can have telegraph and electricity poles moved; contact the service companies about this and ascertain likely costs. If there are buildings on the plot, bear in mind the cost of demolition, including digging out foundations which might be all that's left but not visible. Cost depends on the type of building - a dilapidated shed would cost next to nothing to remove, but a World War Two bunker could cost a fortune. Get quotes from demolition contractors. You need permission from the district council to demolish buildings in a Conservation Area.

ORIENTATION

Check the orientation of the plot - north, south, east or west - as this influences the amount of sun and shade in house and garden. Look at this in relation to trees and neighbouring properties that could cast shadows in your garden. Remember that, if you want to build energy efficiency into your home, a southerly aspect makes the most of the sun's heat and light. When considering orientation, also check the direction of prevailing winds which can have a bearing on the design of your house, as it's better for main doors to be sheltered.

BOUNDARIES

Check the boundaries so that you are clear about exactly what's included in the plot you're buying. Ask the vendor, or his agent, for a copy of the plan from the title deeds which shows the boundaries of legal ownership or download one from the Land Registry website. Old deed plans are often based on out-of-date maps and boundary lines might be drawn so thickly that their precise position is open to argument. Fences and hedges don't always coincide with legal ownership boundaries. If a boundary isn't clear or marked, speak to the vendor first, and possibly to the neighbours, to clarify the position.

Figure 8.3

An urban infill plot constrained by trees, an adjoining blank flank wall and a combination of a sloping end of terrace site and uncertain ground conditions, which could affect structural stability

Avoid boundary disputes as they can be costly and time consuming. Where a boundary is disputed or yet to be defined, get an accurate site survey drawing to form the basis for settling on a solution and get the boundaries pegged out with measurements agreed and recorded. Ordnance Survey plans show where there are physical boundaries but not who owns them. The district council can't help in any boundary disputes, unless they happen to own the adjacent land. Lines marked on previous planning application plans give guidance but have no legal status.

Where the boundary is just a hedge, the centre line is usually taken as the legal boundary. Where there's a hedge and a ditch, the edge of the ditch farthest from the hedge is generally the legal boundary - it's assumed that the land owner first dug the ditch along his boundary then planted the hedge on his own land, on top of the excavated soil.

ADJOINING USES

When assessing your plot, it's also important to check adjoining land uses and the wider surroundings for anything that could spoil your enjoyment of the property and whether the situation could change. Investigate building works of any kind or vacant land with development potential. Make a note of any areas you think might be vulnerable to undesirable change so that you can look into them at the planning department or on the website of the district council. If your first look at a plot was at a weekend, go back and look for schools, businesses or industry that create noise, smells or traffic during the week, especially if they're upwind from your plot. In rural areas consider what it would be like to live downwind from a chicken farm or abattoir. How ever well you know the area, find your plot on the Local Plan or Local Development Framework (LDF) proposals map, which you can look up on-ine, or see either at the district council or at a local library. This will give you an insight into how the area is planned to develop in future. It's always worth finding out why a plot hasn't been built on before, especially if it's been on the market for some time. Ask the vendor or selling agent - there's often a good reason but there might be some physical or legal problem which has inhibited building on the plot. If you're at all suspicious, tell your solicitor and be vigilant when checking all the points covered in this Part of the book.

THE PROPERTY MARKET

At first sight, the current state of the property market might not seem relevant to your assessment of a plot but it can be. Assessing a plot properly takes time and can cost you money. In a busy plot market there might not be time to research everything as thoroughly as you'd like before exchanging contracts, so you need to concentrate on those things that could prevent you building altogether, or could add substantial cost. In a slow property market, where vendors can be desperate to sell, you should be able to load more of the time and cost of assessment on to the vendor and his agent.

CHAPTER 9 ACCESS

A building plot needs vehicular access to a public highway which meets highway safety standards. In almost all cases, this is straightforward, as part of the plot usually fronts on to a road, and a new or existing opening is used to build an access and driveway. Sometimes, though, there's more to the question of access than first meets the eye and failure to provide adequate access can mean failure to build a house. There are two separate aspects to consider - one is the legal right of access to a road, the other is complying with highway authority standards. These are completely separate matters and both must be satisfied.

A new access comprises: a kerb; a crossover (the section of drive that crosses the verge and any footpath) and the drive itself, and usually an on-site turning area for vehicles. Accesses can be single, shared or paired (see Figure 9.1). A shared access is a single drive serving two or more houses. A paired access is where two access points come together at the road frontage creating

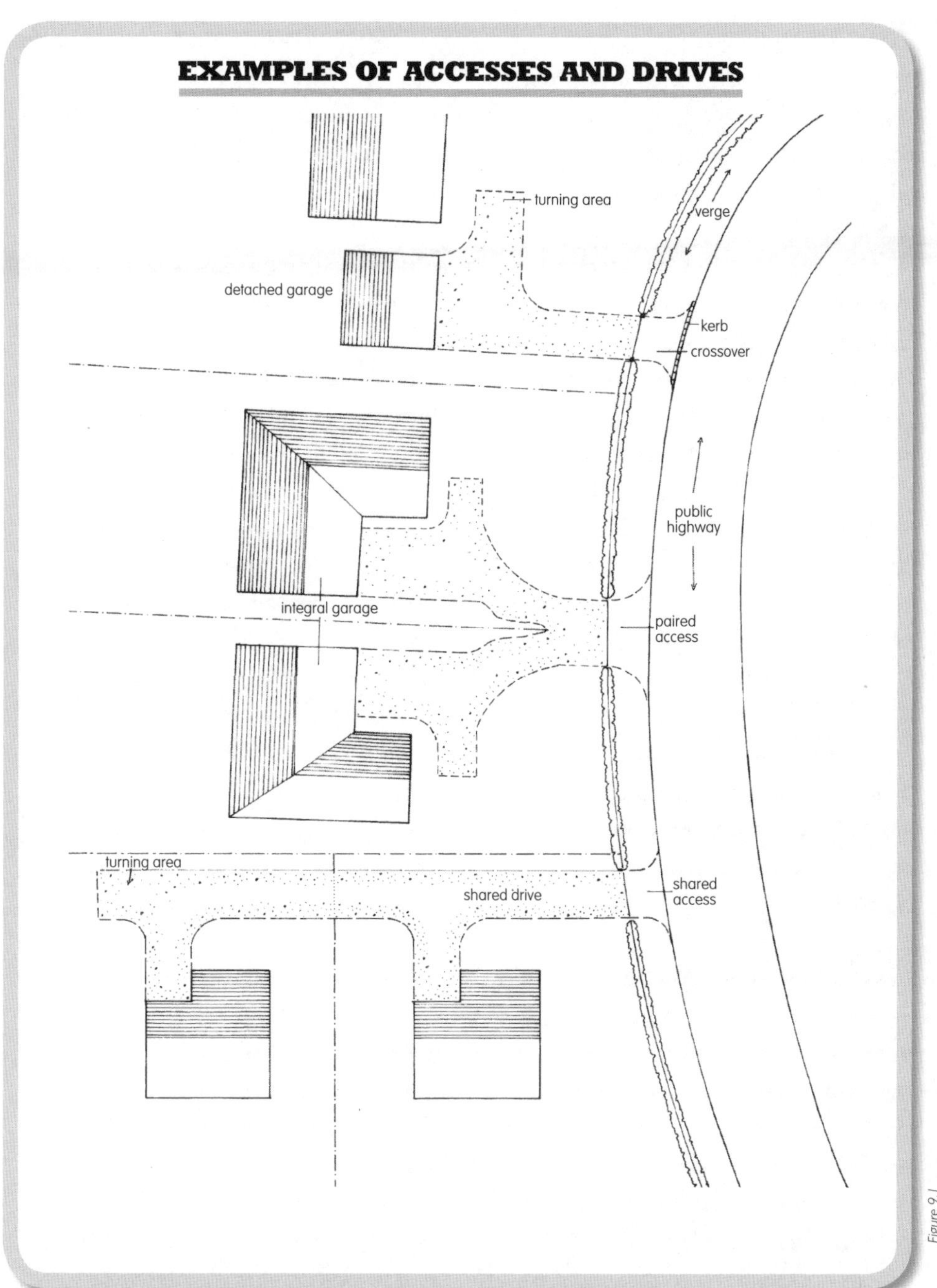

Various access arrangements are possible depending on road conditions and available land

a double width crossover which is shared between the two properties. A paired access is usually used where there's not enough space in each plot to comply with highway authority standards.

Most roads are public adopted highways which means they're owned and maintained by the local highway authority - in England this is normally the county council or, in metropolitan and other single-tier authority areas, the council; in Scotland, the council; in Wales, the county or county borough council; and in Northern Ireland, the Roads Service of the Department for Regional Development. Roads are classified A, B or C; very small roads and estate roads are unclassified. Finally, there are unadopted and private roads. New accesses directly onto motorways and trunk roads aren't permitted.

LEGAL CONSIDERATIONS

When you have planning permission to build a house, and your plot adjoins a public road, you don't need separate permission to get access, although construction details of the crossover will need the highway authority's approval. Where access from a plot would be onto an unadopted or private road, check that there's a right to use that road and who's responsible for its maintenance. Surprisingly, there's often no clear answer and, in these cases, residents whose properties front the private road sometimes group together to share maintenance costs. Alternatively, residents ask the highway authority to adopt the road which they'll generally do only if the road is built to its standards. Making up a road to the required standard can be very expensive, or impossible if the existing road is too narrow and residents are unwilling to lose strips of their front gardens. Where the precise ownership of a road can't be discovered, you can take out insurance cover against a challenge to your right to use the road in future. Different ownerships of sections of road are often obvious on the ground because of changes in surfacing - beware of a neat tarmac road that gives way to hardcore and potholes just short of the plot.

VERGES

Another area where land ownership is often unclear is at the roadside verge. In most cases, where a plot fronts a road, any land between the edge of the road and a plot boundary is also owned and maintained by the local highway authority. This might be grass verge or pavement and you're allowed to cross it without having to pay for a right. Where there's any doubt, ask the highway authority to confirm the extent of publicly maintained road in the vicinity of the site.

COMMON LAND

Access to a plot could run over common land, which might be in one ownership but subject to various rights granted to other people. Although these might be of the 'right to graze three pigs and a gaggle of geese between the months of July and October' variety, they can still prevent you getting access. Take advice on the implications of this from your solicitor.

RANSOM STRIPS

Where there's land in somebody else's ownership between your land and the public highway, there could be a ransom strip (see Figure 9.2). There's no automatic right to cross such land unless you get, or the plot already has, a specific right of access. A ransom strip can be a few inches wide but, in such a case, an inch is as good as a mile. The owner of the ransom strip in effect controls whether or not you can build on your plot, and hence the 'ransom'. Ransoms often exist where the roadside verge is in another ownership, which might be the parish or district council or a private individual. It could even be owned by the council that is the highway authority, but not be part of the public highway, and so there's no automatic right to cross it. It's your solicitors' job to check that you can get access to the plot and their normal investigations during your purchase should show up any defects or problems. Make sure your solicitors' searches include not just the plot itself but also a strip of access road outside it. If you find there's difficulty over access, normally leave it to the vendor to sort out and don't buy the plot until it's resolved.

Overcoming a ransom strip usually means buying the land in question or a right of access over it but there's nothing to say that an owner has to sell. Anyone who realises the importance of the ransom strip will probably want some of the development value of the plot. 'Development value' means what the land is worth as a building plot, less its value for its existing use as garden or field. In a well known and often quoted legal case, Stokes v. Cambridge (1961), a third of the development value was paid for

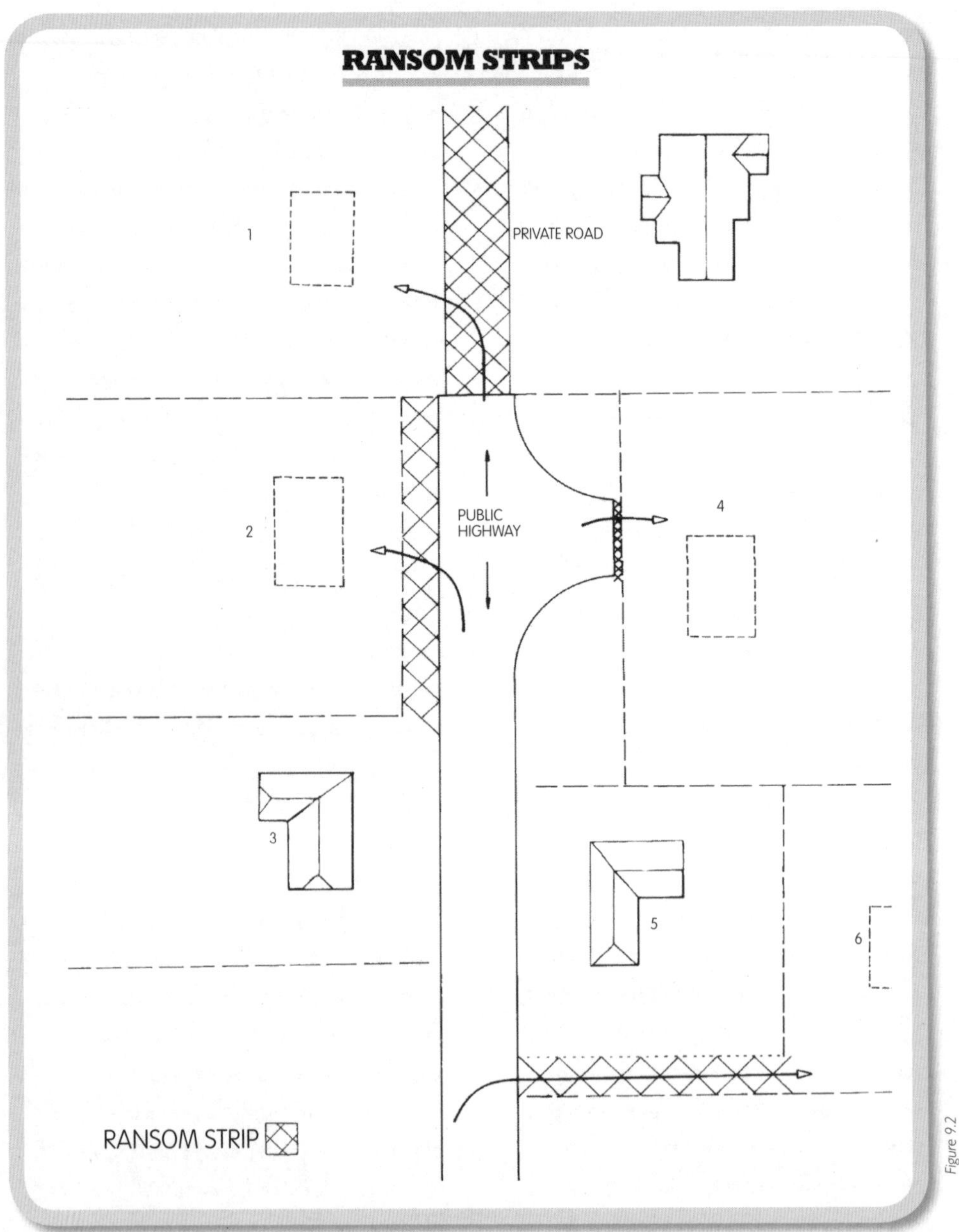

The most common situations where ransom strips arise are (plot 1) access over a length of private road, (plot 2) roadside verge in the ownership of house no. 3, (plot 4) a strip of land deliberately kept by a previous owner, and (plot 6) access through the garden of house no. 5

an access. The amount of ransom money paid is, though, a matter for negotiation and depends on whether there are alternative ways to get access. Buying a ransom strip shouldn't, however, affect the overall price you pay for a plot. Either the vendor pays the ransom or, if you have to pay say a £10,000 ransom for access, you reduce your bid for the plot by £10,000. Where a ransom strip has to be bought out, your solicitors might need the backing of a surveyor or valuer to provide valuations. If the owner of the ransom refuses to sell, your only option is to find a different plot.

HIGHWAY STANDARDS

Highway authority standards concern: visibility at the point of access onto the highway; construction of the kerb and crossover; width and length of the drive; and parking and turning facilities. Highway standards are applied and assessed when planning applications are made for new houses. The highway authority comments on access and turning arrangements and sets out its requirements, which the district council can include in a condition when giving planning permission. So, where planning permission has already been given, assuming that you can comply with any highway conditions attached to it (and subject to having the necessary legal rights), you can go ahead and build the access. If the plot doesn't have planning permission, check that you can meet highway standards.

There must be clear visibility at the point of access onto the highway so that approaching drivers can see an emerging vehicle, and vice versa. This can rule out new accesses near sharp bends, near the crest of a hill or where there are double white lines in the centre of the road, indicating that forward visibility is poor. There must be a visibility splay at each side of an access, that is, areas that must be kept free of obstructions so that lines of sight are clear (see Figure 9.3). The drive of a single house usually requires a clear view up and down the road from a point 2.4 m (8 ft) back from the edge of the road. In areas with light traffic or slow speeds, this point can be a minimum of 2.0 m (6ft 6ins). The distance for which a driver must be able to see along the road varies according to the type of road and speed of traffic. It can be as little as 11 m (36ft 6ins) in each direction, where traffic is very slow-moving, and more than 200 m (666 ft) where traffic is fast-moving.

Check visibility by taking two-and-

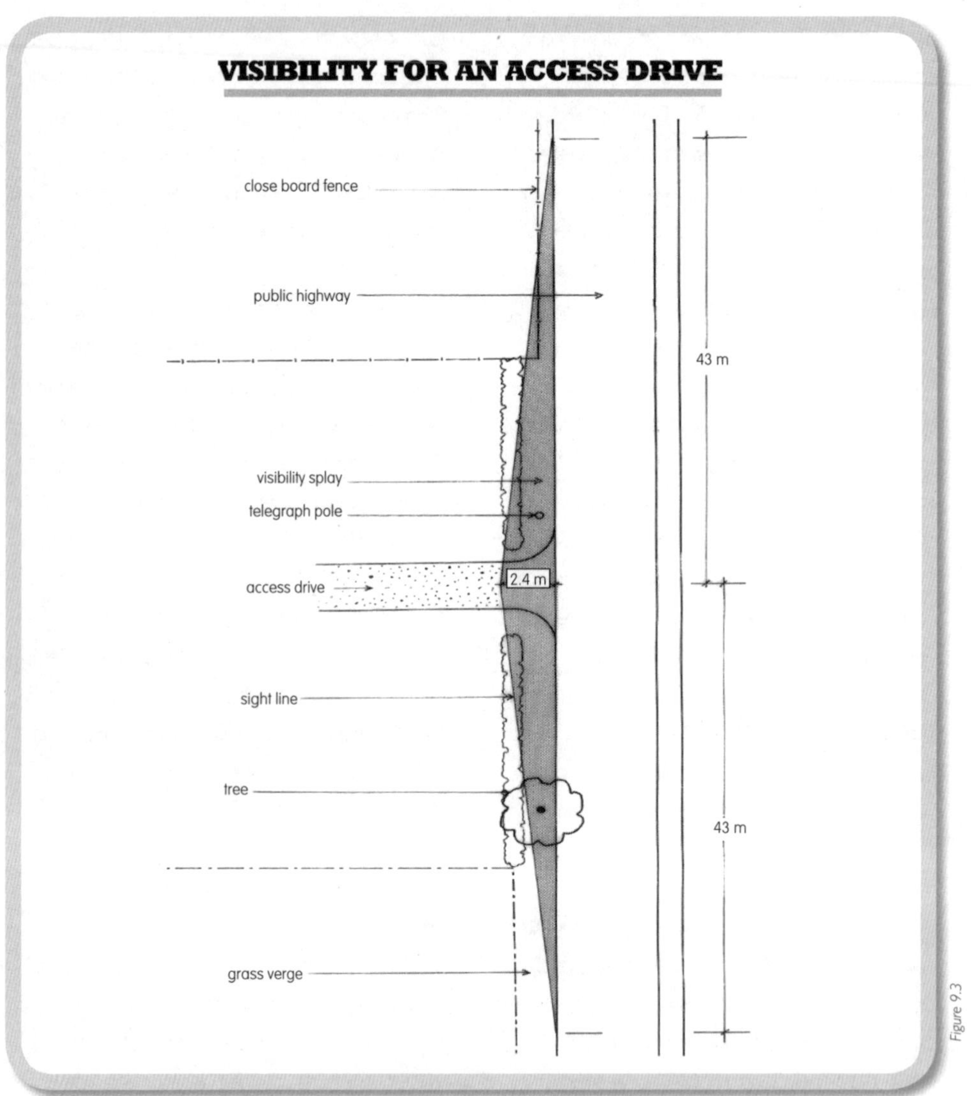

This is a typical visibility splay needed for a new house in a 30 mile-an-hour speed limit – watch out for adjoining fences, hedges, telegraph poles, and trees which could block lines of sight and have to be removed

a-half paces back from the edge of the road, at the centre of the access point, and then looking up and down the road. A neighbour's hedge or fence could block the view, or a tree, telegraph pole, road sign or bus shelter might be in just the wrong spot. Where visibility is blocked, find out who owns the hedge, fence or obstruction, and whether you can have it moved and at what cost. An obstruction which prevents adequate visibility can jeopardise planning permission and a sharp owner could hold you to ransom. Don't assume that street trees can necessarily be felled or cut back, they may be protected by a TPO. If bus shelters, pillar boxes or telegraph poles must be moved, you'll have to pay the cost. Before you decide to buy a plot, make sure you know what any such costs would be.

Parking and turning standards vary according to the size of house and type of road. As a general rule, outside housing estates there must be sufficient turning space on site so that cars don't have to back out onto the road. If your drive is long (over about 45 m), you'll probably need a minimum width of 3.5 m plus a lorry-turning area so that fire engines and/or dustcarts can enter and turn around but ascertain the local requirements. Note, at this stage, that building regulations permission can be refused where fire engines can't get access to a house with a long drive. This could stop you building, even though planning permission might have been given.

Where you can't comply with highway standards, and highway safety would be threatened as a result, the district council is likely to refuse planning permission. Highway standards aren't always rigidly applied and, if your scheme is acceptable in all other respects, there might be some flexibility, although planning applications are often refused for access and highway safety reasons. If you encounter access problems, get professional advice from a planning consultant or highway engineer.

CHAPTER 10

SERVICES

Investigate services at an early stage in your assessment of a plot, not as an afterthought when you've bought it. Look into the availability and cost of connection to the main services - drainage, water, electricity, gas and telephone. Where main services aren't available, you should explore alternatives. Foul and surface water drainage has to be approved by the district council, which can refuse planning permission for a new house if the proposed drainage isn't satisfactory. Services running under or over a site can be an obstacle to building, so you also need to find out their locations for this reason.

FOUL DRAINAGE

The first choice for foul drainage is usually a connection to the nearest public foul sewer. Sewer records, based on Ordnance Survey maps, showing the position, depth and size of drains are kept either by the drainage company or by the district council (see Figure 10.1). Levels at manholes are marked on the record including a cover level (top of the manhole cover) and an invert level (bottom of the sewer pipe) and the difference between the two gives the depth of the sewer. Contact the drainage company to find out how or where to see or get a copy of the record, for which many make a charge. Find out where the nearest sewer is and ask for confirmation that you can connect to it.

Connection to a public foul sewer can usually be made where there's a fall in level from house to sewer and the sewer has adequate capacity. If the sewer is uphill, a pump system can be used which might increase cost but now, with the development of small bore systems, pumping is more viable. While investigating sewers, check on connection charges and take account of the distance to the sewer and whether you have to cross a road to it as these factors add to the cost. Sometimes a public foul sewer can only be reached by crossing someone else's land or connection has to be made via a private sewer. In either case, the necessary rights have to be negotiated with and acquired from the owner in order to make a connection. In some areas at certain times, when you apply for planning permission for a new house, you'll meet a drainage embargo which stops you connecting into the public sewers because the drains or the sewage treatment plant have reached capacity and need replacing or upgrading. If a plot is affected by a drainage embargo, talk to the drainage authority and district council to find out how long it might last and whether there's a way of getting around it.

Where there's no public sewer available, investigate private disposal systems - sewage treatment plant, septic tank or sealed cesspool. A septic tank is a large container, sunk into the ground usually at least 15 m (50 ft) from the house, which needs emptying about once a year. Septic tanks require an area of land, well away from the house, into which the treated water drains and, if the plot itself isn't large enough, you'd need to negotiate the use of some adjoining land. You must get approval for a septic tank from the Environment Agency in England and Wales, the Rivers Purification Boards in Scotland or the Water Service of the Department of the Environment in Northern Ireland. In areas of impervious clay, where there's a high ground water table or where there's a river or stream nearby, a septic tank might not be allowed. The modern alternative to a septic tank is a mini sewage treatment plant and various models are made, suitable to serve individual houses. Unlike a septic tank, the water discharged can usually go direct into a watercourse but check with the Environment Agency, Rivers Purification Board or Water Service whether these systems are allowed in your area. A cesspool is simply a large sealed tank that has to be emptied six to twelve times a year by tanker for which you need to provide access. Look into the likely cost of emptying, especially in remote areas.

SURFACE WATER DRAINAGE

Surface water drainage takes care of the water from the roofs of the house and garage and possibly from drives and other hard surfaces. Soakaways are commonly used to disperse surface water and consist of a large pit filled with rubble from which surface water seeps into the surrounding soil. The size and number of soakaways you'll need varies with the size of house and type of soil. In areas where the soil is impervious or the water table is high, soakaways aren't permitted or are only allowed after percolation tests have been carried out. Speak to the building control section of the district council about surface water drainage, as they know the local ground conditions and can tell you about likely difficulties.

If your plot is next to, or crossed by, a ditch or stream, a piped outfall discharging surface water directly into it might be permitted. In areas liable to flood or where you build as part of a group of houses, you can be asked to provide flood prevention measures, like a holding tank to take the first rush of water after a downpour. In urban areas there are sometimes public surface water sewers into which you can connect and, in very limited cases, you're allowed to connect to the public foul sewer. Road drains aren't public surface water sewers and you'd need the highway authority's permission to connect to them. As with foul sewers, if you have to cross someone else's land to make a connection, you'll probably have to pay.

Many self-build houses now incorporate recycling rain or 'grey' water for use in flushing toilets and outside taps. Where you want to store surface water for use in your

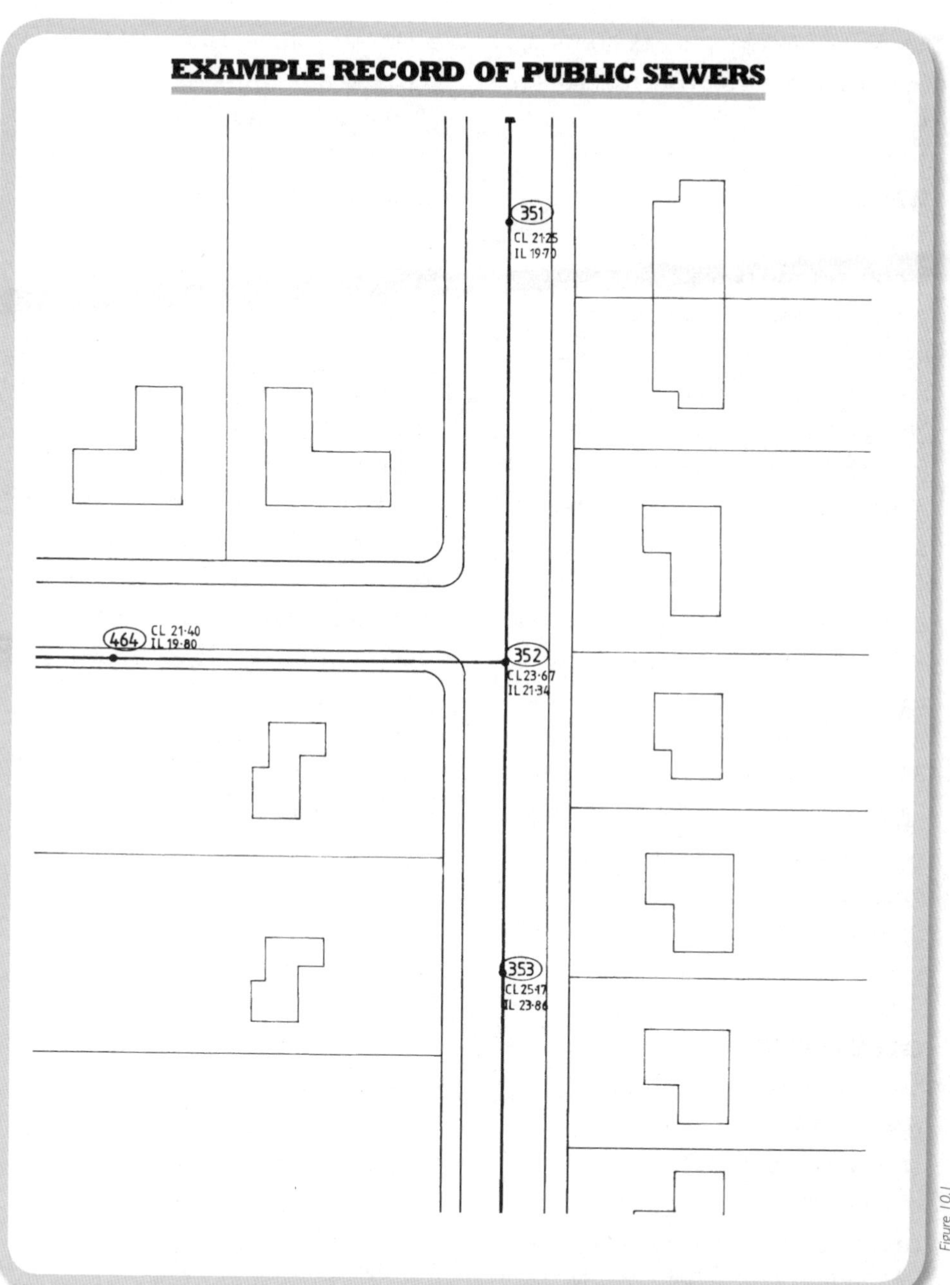

Plans like this show the position of public sewers and the location and levels of manholes, similar plans exist for surface water sewers, gas and water pipes and electricity cables

house or garden, this won't affect the eventual means of drainage for any excess.

WATER

The local water company has records of the position and size of water mains. These usually run under roads and, in most cases, are readily available but check connection charges as they can be high. Where a water main isn't available, ask the water company about the cost of laying a supply to your property. They're obliged to do this but you have to contribute to the cost which, if the nearest main is miles away, is likely to be prohibitive. In those circumstances, speak to the water company about alternative water sources, like bore holes, streams and springs, and whether you'd need an abstraction licence. Find out the cost of putting in and running a private system.

OTHER SERVICES

Mains electricity is widely available, gas less so. The gas and electricity supply companies can give you details of the nearest supply and tell you whether a connection can be made and at what cost. Most companies charge for supplying this information. If mains gas isn't available, bulk storage tanks are an alternative. If you want to use oil, this also needs a storage tank. Decide where these could be put on a plot and how you would get access for refilling. If possible, position tanks so that they can be filled by a hose, while the delivery tanker stays on the road, as not all private drives can take the weight of a fully laden lorry. In remote areas the cost of a telephone connection can be high if there are no existing lines nearby. Check the likely cost with BT plc if you can't see telephone lines anywhere near the plot. Broadband, too, can be a bit hit and miss in rural areas so check what connection speeds are available if a high speed connection is important to you.

CHAPTER TEN ● SERVICES

CHAPTER 11

PLANNING PERMISSION

A piece of land only becomes a building plot if it has planning permission. If you want to build a new home, convert an existing building or add significantly to an existing house, you need planning permission. Building without planning permission or failing to comply with the conditions on a planning permission can lead to drastic action being taken by a district council - new houses built without permission are bulldozed to the ground from time to time. Don't buy a plot unless you're certain of getting planning permission for the house you want to build. This chapter explains the basics of planning permission and tells you the essential points to look for. The right way to make a planning application and what to do if it's refused is fully explained in a companion volume to this book, How To Get Planning Permission.

Planning permission is given by district councils. The district council has a planning department which deals with planning applications and queries and which keeps planning records. Planning departments employ professional staff, called planning or development control officers, who assess planning applications, advise planning committees and decide uncontentious planning applications. More controversial applications are decided by planning committees made up of councillors, who are lay people elected onto the council. All decisions in Northern Ireland are made by divisional planning officers after consultation with district councillors.

The terms 'planning permission', 'planning approval' and 'planning consent' all have exactly the same meaning. Planning permission relates to a site and not to the person who makes the application. You don't have to own a plot in order to make a planning application. If a plot already has planning permission, this doesn't stop you making another application for a different design or layout. Planning permission doesn't mean that the owner has to build the house or guarantee that a house can be built, as there can still be legal or practical reasons that prevent it. There are two kinds of planning permission - outline permission (permission in principle in Scotland) and detailed or full permission. Detailed permission includes all the details of the proposal - size, style, layout, position within the plot, materials, access, and foul and surface water disposal arrangements. Detailed planning permission is normally given subject to conditions, which sometimes specify further things that have to be approved before construction starts, like a landscaping scheme and samples of building materials.

Outline planning permission establishes the principle that a house can be built on a plot, leaving the design and layout to be settled later. An outline planning permission indicates the approximate dimensions of the house, might specify the type of house and can be subject to a wide range of conditions, including the position of the access and the height or size of the house. When outline planning permission is given, details of layout, scale, appearance, access and landscaping (collectively known as 'reserved matters') can be put forward to the district council in a separate type of application, called a reserved matters application. When both outline planning permission and reserved matters have been approved, the two together are the

SCRIDDLE BOROUGH COUNCIL

Application number GR/2009/00877

TOWN & COUNTRY PLANNING ACT 1990

OUTLINE PLANNING PERMISSION

Mr K & Mrs M Frumble
c/o Spicer Deade Planning Consultants
Cruckett Hill Street
Grimston FG26 9SK

Scriddle Borough Council in pursuance of powers under the above Act hereby PERMIT

Erection of dwelling and garage
at Land Adjoining 124 Stinchcombe Road, Tressle

in accordance with your application received on 1st May 2009 and plans (listed below) which form part of the application

Site Plan reference SD/C272 received 01.05.2009

1 Condition Approval of the details of the access; appearance; landscaping; layout; and scale (hereinafter called the 'reserved matters') shall be obtained from the Local Planning Authority in writing before any development is commenced.

1 Reason To enable the Local Planning Authority to control the development in detail and to comply with Section 92 of the Town & Country Planning Act 1990.

2 Condition Application for approval of reserved matters shall be made to the Local Planning Authority before the expiration of three years from the date of this permission.

2 Reason To enable the Local Planning Authority to control the development in detail and to comply with Section 92 of the Town & Country Planning Act 1990.

A decision notice granting outline planning permission sets out basic information

3 Condition The development hereby permitted shall be begun not later than the expiration of two years from the final approval of the reserved matters or, in the case of approval in different dates, the final approval of the last such matter to be approved.

3 Reason To enable the Local Planning Authority to control the development in detail and to comply with Section 92 of the Town & Country Planning Act 1990.

4 Condition Details of the type, colour and texture of all materials to be used for the external surfaces of the building(s) shall be submitted to and approved in writing by the Local Planning Authority prior to the commencement of the development to which this permission relates. The development shall be carried out in accordance with the approved details.

4 Reason In the interests of visual amenity in accordance with Policy EN14 of the Scriddle Local Plan 1999.

5 Condition No development shall take place until full details of both hard and soft landscape works have been submitted to and approved in writing by the Local Planning Authority and these works shall be carried out as approved.

5 Reason To enhance the appearance of the development in accordance with Policy EN10 contained in the Scriddle Local Plan 1999.

Note to applicant
The Local Planning Authority has had regard to the provisions of the Development Plan so far as material to the application and to all other material considerations.

Deidre Swonk

Development Control Manager
Operational Services Directorate

Date 30th June 2009
SCRIDDLE BOROUGH COUNCIL

Figure 11.1

on the application and the conditions to which the permission is subject

A location plan is submitted with every planning application defining the extent of the site and any other land owned by the applicant

equivalent of a detailed permission.

STUDYING THE PLANNING PERMISSION

Study the planning application and permission early on when you assess a plot. The vendors or their agent ought to be able to show you or give you copies but, if not, you can view them on the council's website or see and buy copies at the planning department of the district council. You can arrange to have copies sent to you through the post, for which there's usually a charge, and you need to give the application reference number.

An outline planning application and permission consists of the application form, design and access statement, location plan identifying the plot, indicative site layout plan and the council's decision notice with conditions listed (see Figures 11.1 and 11.2). Any additional detailed plans submitted with the outline application for illustrative purposes aren't strictly speaking part of the permission. Don't rely on them as an indication of what the council will allow you to build. A detailed application and permission includes full site layout plans, floor plans and elevations as well as the application form, design and access statement, location plan and decision notice (see Figures 11.3 and 11.4). All approved plans and documents should be stamped by the district council. Where plans have been amended or revised, make sure you see the most recent versions.

First check the date of the planning permission. Detailed planning permission expires after three years, unless work is started within that period. Outline planning permission expires after three years, unless an application for approval of reserved matters is made within that time. Work must start within two years of the approval of reserved matters. If a vendor claims that a planning permission is still valid because work had started, check what was done, when and ask the vendor to get the district council to confirm, at least, in writing but, better still, in a formal lawful development certificate, that it agrees the works did get under way and the planning permission hasn't expired. If the permission hasn't got long to run, you can't assume it will be automatically renewed. Ideally, get the vendor to renew it before you commit to buy.

Next look at conditions listed on the decision notice to make sure you're able and willing to meet them, as the council can take action against you if you don't comply with conditions. Typically conditions cover:

- time limits - building work to start within three years
- external materials - samples of building materials to be approved by the district council
- car parking and turning space - defined areas to be kept clear
- access - sight lines, construction of kerb and crossover, layout of drive

Amble Point District Council

TOWN AND COUNTRY PLANNING ACT 1990
Town and Country Planning (General Development Procedure) Order 1995

PLANNING PERMISSION

Applicant:	Mr F & Mrs O Punt 3 Bistow Lane Pogswood NC3 6TG	Agent: Deer Spade Planning Consultants 29 Regent Drive Pinderhead NC9 7QA

LOCATION:	Land rear of 5 Peewit Court, Haggleback
PROPOSAL:	Erection of four bedroom dwelling and garage
APPLICATION NO:	09/00598/FUL
DATE RECEIVED:	29th September 2009
DRAWING NO(s):	LOCATION PLAN; DS/323/1; DS/323/2; DS/323/3A;

The Council has given consideration to the application and plans as specified above, and hereby gives notice of its decision to GRANT PLANNING PERMISSION subject to the following conditions:-

1 The development hereby permitted shall be begun before the expiration of three years from the date of this permission.

2 Prior to commencement of the development hereby permitted, a schedule and samples of materials and finishes to be used for the external walls and roofs shall be submitted to, and approved in writing by, the local planning authority.

3 Before the building hereby permitted is occupied, a close board wooden fence 1.8 metres in height shall be erected and thereafter maintained, along the north-eastern boundary of the site.

4 All window openings in the south-west and north-east flank walls of the permitted building shall be glazed with obscured glass only.

A decision notice granting detailed planning permission contains

Reasons:-

1 In order to comply with Section 91(1) of the Town and Country Planning Act 1990 as amended by Section 51 of the planning and Compulsory Purchase Act 2004.
2 To secure a satisfactory external appearance in the interests of amenity.
3 To preserve the privacy and amenity of the adjoining residential property.
4 To preserve the privacy and amenity of the adjoining residential property.

The Development Plan policies taken into account in deciding this application are listed below. The full text of the policies may be inspected at the Council's offices.
DEV2, DEV45, DEV47

Reason(s) for this Decision

1 The proposal demonstrates reasonable compliance with the relevant policies of the Development Plan and there are no other material considerations.

Date: 28 November 2009

Signed:

Driscoll Jolly

DRISCOLL JOLLY
Director of Sustainable Communities

IMPORTANT - YOUR ATTENTION IS DRAWN TO THE NOTES ATTACHED

Figure 11.3

the conditions and gives brief reasons why permission was granted

- trees, shrubs and hedges - restrictions on felling, protection during construction
- landscaping - scheme to be approved by the district council, maintenance of landscaping schemes
- drainage - details to be approved by the district council

Watch particularly for conditions that require other work to be done before the house is built, like an access to be built with clear sight lines or a building to be demolished. Make sure you can get all the necessary rights and consents to fulfil these conditions. There are limits on what councils are supposed to include in conditions but this doesn't stop them trying it on. One fairly common example you might come across is a limit on the times when the council says building work can take place, such as no work before 9 am or after 6 pm on Monday to Friday, and no working at weekends. This sort of condition shouldn't be placed on a permission unless there are very exceptional circumstances. If you don't fully understand the conditions, speak to your solicitor, a planning officer or a planning consultant. Planning permission can also be granted subject to a legal agreement (see

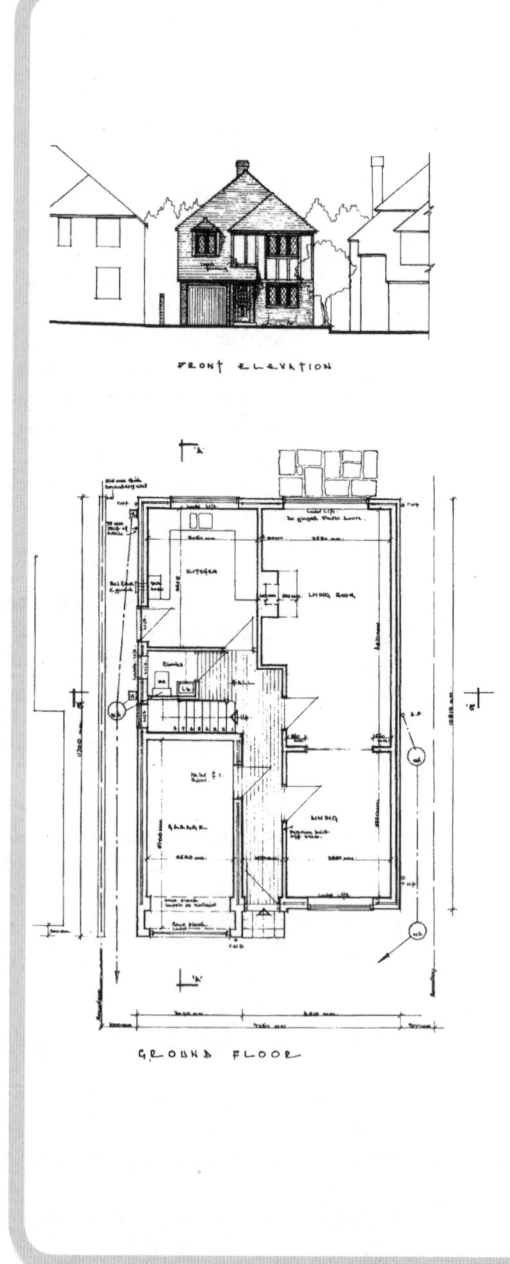

Detailed planning applications are accompanied

DETAILED PLANNING PERMISSION DRAWINGS

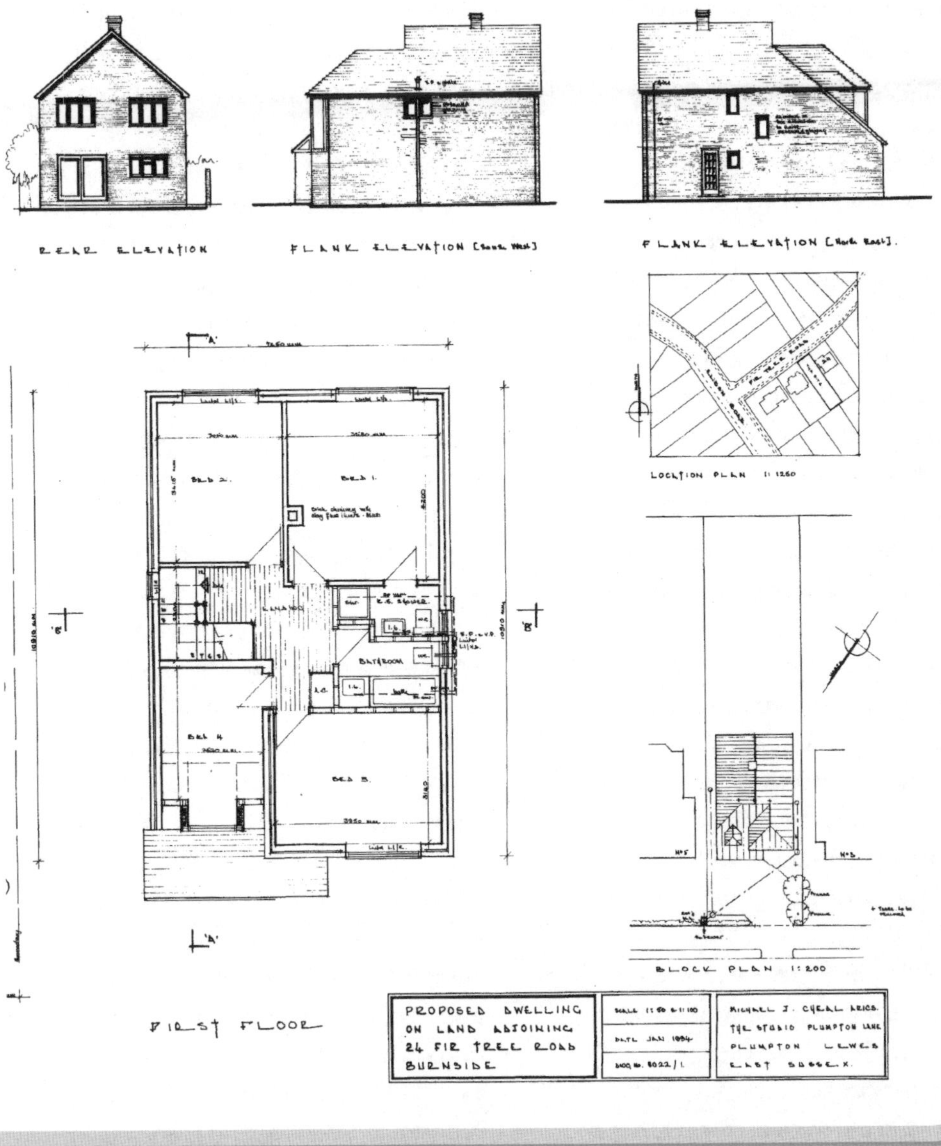

Figure 11.4

by drawings showing the location, site layout, floor plans and elevations of the building

Chapter 13).

Study the application plans to check the boundaries of the application site and the ownership boundaries of the plot are exactly the same. You might not be able to carry out the planning permission, if you don't own all the land and can't build according to the plan.

Where you buy a plot with detailed planning permission, it's unlikely that you'll want to build the house exactly as shown in the permission, in which case you need to make a new application for your own design and layout. If your plot has outline planning permission, you can choose between making a reserved matters application or a new detailed application (see above). Where your house-type is consistent with the outline permission and you can comply with the conditions, apply for approval of reserved matters. The advantage of this is that the district council only considers the detail of the house, not the principle. When a detailed application is made, the whole question of whether a house should be built on the plot at all could, in theory, be reviewed.

The safest course is to get planning permission for the house you intend to build before you buy the plot but, since this takes a few months, there's not always time. In this case, find out whether you're likely to get permission. Call in at the planning department and ask to see the file for the existing planning permission. Not all councils are happy to hand you their files, although most are, but the planning application and plans, decision notice and the planning officer's report on the application (see Figure 11.5) are all public documents you're entitled to see. Find the officer's report in the file - some are an inadequate few lines but others are comprehensive and so very useful to help you assess whether you can get planning permission for what you want. Good reports describe the application, the planning history of the site and local planning policies relevant to the application. If the plot is in or near a Conservation Area, an Area of Outstanding Natural Beauty or National Scenic Area in Scotland, a Site of Special Scientific Interest or has protected trees on it, these facts should be noted. The council consults neighbours, the parish council, highway authority and others and their comments are included in the officer's report. The report summarises the planning officer's views and highlights any areas of concern which give you useful pointers for the sort of proposal that will be allowed.

Occasionally you find the planning officer recommended refusal of the application but planning permission was nevertheless granted by the committee. This suggests that you might have to deal with a less than enthusiastic planning officer when you put forward your detailed scheme. Ask the planning officer why permission was given.

If the existing planning permission is detailed, look for anything in the report which indicates whether the district council will like or dislike your scheme, as opposed to the one approved. For example, the officer could have said the scheme was acceptable because the proposed house had a low roof line and the mellow tones of the clay tiles made it relatively unobtrusive. This gives you a clear idea of the sort of design that's likely to be approved.

While you're looking at the planning file of the plot, read any letters from objectors or supporters and from the various consultees. It's interesting, of course, to know which neighbours objected to an application but, more important, the letters might alert you to possible boundary or other disputes, or to the existence of a restrictive covenant.

Some or all of the above research might be possible on-line, via the council's website. Bear in mind though that on-line records aren't always complete. A look through the case file can unearth hand written notes for example that might reveal useful information not formally on the record.

PLANNING OFFICER

As well as looking up the file on the existing planning permission, speak to a planning officer about the site and the sort of house you want to build. The officer can usually give you a good idea whether your house would get planning permission or what sort of scheme the council would want to see. What the planning officer says at a meeting, or even in a letter, can't commit the council when an application is made, so be guided by his comments but don't rely on them totally. Telephone the planning department to find out about its procedure for pre-application advice, as it varies somewhat from council to council and some charge for meetings and advice. Many require you to send in any plans, drawings or sketches of your house in advance of a meeting

EXAMPLE PLANNING OFFICER'S REPORT

Application no:	09/01124/OUT
Application type:	Outline Planning Application
Proposal:	Erection of a detached house
Address:	52 Slanting Drive, Buckleford
Applicant:	Mr & Mrs G Knockerage

CONSULTATIONS

Neighbouring properties: three letters objecting to over-development, loss of trees, dangerous access.

Buckleford Conservation Group: object, out of character, inappropriate infill, tree felling.

Borough Engineer: removal of part of frontage hedge required to create adequate visibility to north.

POLICIES

Borough Core Strategy: S3

Development Control Policies: H2, H3, ENV7

SITE AND SURROUNDINGS

The application site extends to 0.07 hectares of level grass. It is bounded by established hedgerows and trees on the east and west boundaries and close board fence on the north and south. There is a group of protected trees in the south-east corner. The area is characterised by detached houses on either side of Slant Drive in mature grounds. To the north, 54 Slant Drive is a two storey brick dwelling with one ground floor window facing the application site. On the other side Boggle Cottage is a rendered, chalet style dwelling set 5 metres from the side boundary. This dwelling has a kitchen window in the ground floor and a small dormer window serving a bedroom at first floor level.

SITE HISTORY

Application 99/786/FULL for the erection of a block of four flats was refused in 1999.

PROPOSAL

The application proposes to build a detached house with a new access to Slant Drive being created. The application is in outline with all matters reserved so the design and layout does not fall to be considered at this

The planning officer's report describes the proposal and all the considerations in the

stage. The application indicates a building of 5.0-6.0 metres in width and 7.0-7.5 metres deep with a maximum height of 7.0 metres. Illustrative drawings submitted with the application show a two-storey dwelling set in line with adjoining houses between 4.0-6.0 metres from the side boundaries.

ASSESSMENT

Housing development is acceptable in principle on this site which lies within the settlement as defined in the Proposals Map. The density of development is slightly higher than that prevailing in the immediate vicinity but not to such a degree as to cause loss of amenity or harm to character. Although only in outline, concern is expressed over the likely proximity of the rear of the house to the protected trees. The submitted site layout plan, whilst not forming part of the formal application, demonstrates that a dwelling can be accommodated satisfactorily outside the root protection zone as defined in the submitted arboricultural report. Formation of the new access would require the loss of a length of the frontage hedge to meet visibility standards of the Borough Engineer. Appropriate landscaping conditions can be attached to a permission requiring the replacement of the hedge behind the visibility splay. The relationship with adjoining properties would be acceptable and a condition can be attached to ensure any side windows are obscure glazed to protect privacy of neighbours. Notwithstanding the local objections, the amount of development and effect on trees are not considered strong enough reasons to warrant refusal of this application. The proposal is considered to meet the criteria of Core Strategy policy S3 and Development Control Policies H2, H3 and ENV7 and so can be permitted.

RECOMMENDATION

Grant outline planning subject to the following conditions:

1 Approval of reserved matters
2 Access details to be approved
3 Landscaping scheme to be submitted including replanting of frontage hedge
4 Side windows to be obscure glazed and no insertion of side windows without prior approval by local planning authority
5 Drainage details to be approved

Figure 11.5

case and ends with a recommendation on whether planning permission should be given but others have a duty planning officer system where you can just turn up and get advice. As a rule, the more senior the officer is and the more information you provide in advance, the more reliable will be the advice you're given. At a meeting ask what constraints might affect the design or site layout and whether he feels that your house-type is right for the site. If the officer has objections, discuss them and ask whether they're so significant that planning permission would be turned down. Judging the reaction of a planning officer to a scheme and then deciding what action to take as a result is best done in the light of experience. If in doubt take professional advice.

PROFESSIONAL ADVICE

Whether to get professional help with planning permission depends on your circumstances. If there's a choice of plots in your area of search, it might be easier simply to avoid ones with planning problems. Planning rules and restrictions are very complex, it's better to consult someone who knows the subject, than to get caught out or to just rely on what a planning officer tells you. If you don't have a lot of time to spend on researching the planning situation, use a consultant to do it for you. Where you know that your plans are going to be contentious, get advice to give yourself the maximum chance of success. The requirements for planning applications are now so onerous that it's hard for non-professionals to make them. If you find a piece of land without permission, or without permission for the sort of house you want to build, you can commission a report on planning potential. This will tell you whether you're likely to get permission and how best to go about it. Decide whether your budget can stand the additional professional fees. Spending hundreds of pounds might stop you making a mistake that costs thousands or mean the difference between building your ideal home or not.

Before paying for professional help, you could get the views of people involved in your project. If you're buying through estate agents, ask what they've to say. Agents who sell plots in the area might know something about local planning policies and what else has been given planning permission. Don't forget that the agent is working for the vendor and has an interest in getting you to buy. Where you're going to buy a house from a self-build package company, ask if it has in-house staff who can help. If your problem is straightforward, these people might be able to help but, if it's more complicated, get specialist advice.

If your planning application looks like it will be very straight forward and you only need a basic planning application and drawings prepared, use a building surveyor, architect or architectural technician. If you need advice on getting planning permission, what planning conditions mean, what the planning officer has told you, whether you're likely to get permission for your house or your planning application might be involved or tricky, go to a planning consultant. Planning consultants are either chartered surveyors (MRICS or FRICS) or chartered town planners (MRTPI or FRTPI). Chartered Planning and Development Surveyors specialise in planning and development and have a broad understanding of the subject, including the relationship between planning and values. Most Chartered Town Planner consultants trained and worked in local government before leaving to enter private practice. Some people turn to their own local solicitors because of the apparent semi-legal nature of planning but few are specialists in getting planning permission or in dealing with planning practice, policy and procedure.

CHAPTER 12

PLANNING RESTRICTIONS

Apart from the need for planning permission from the district council, there are a number of planning restrictions which can influence what you build on a plot. Where a plot is affected by these, you must look into the implications for your particular scheme.

AGRICULTURAL TIES

Agricultural ties limit the occupancy of a house; they occur in the countryside where planning permission is given for a house specifically for someone working in agriculture. Agriculture includes horticulture and forestry and so covers all manner of farms, small holdings, nurseries and market gardens. A plot with such a restriction can be tied in two ways and one or both might apply. First, planning permission to build a house can include a condition limiting occupation to 'a person solely or mainly working, or last working, in the locality in agriculture or forestry, or a widow or widower of such a person and to any resident dependants'. Second, a building plot can be tied to a farm, preventing the plot from being sold, or the occupation of the house restricted, through a legally binding document called a 'planning obligation', looked at in Chapter 13. If you build a house on a plot with an agricultural tie and don't come within the definition of who can occupy it, the district council can stop you living there. It's sometimes possible to get round an agricultural occupancy condition but this is only likely where you could get planning permission for a house anyway. You're unlikely to get a condition taken off a plot in the countryside, outside a village. If you can't satisfy the occupancy restriction or can't get a new planning permission without an agricultural tie, don't buy the plot. If you find a sub-standard house with an agricultural tie to demolish and rebuild, it's possible, but not easy, to have the restriction lifted. Again, don't commit yourself to buy until you have planning permission.

ARTICLE 4 DIRECTIONS

Many items of minor building work, which would otherwise need planning permission, are automatically allowed by a government order. This is a practical necessity, preventing district councils being burdened with planning applications for all small alterations and extensions to houses, and for greenhouses, sheds, fences and patios in gardens. These automatic rights (known as 'permitted development') can be taken away by district councils through an Article 4 Direction. You can find out if a plot is affected by an Article 4 Direction from the district council or this may come to light in your solicitors' searches before you buy a plot. Article 4 Directions are very rare and used mainly in Conservation Areas where district councils want greater control over all types of building. This doesn't mean you're not allowed, for example, to build a shed in your garden or put up a new fence, rather that you need planning permission to do so. If a plot is in an area covered by an Article 4 Direction, ask a planning officer to explain exactly what's restricted. Do-it-yourself enthusiasts might find having to get planning permission for various projects costly and time consuming.

TREE PRESERVATION ORDERS

District councils can make Tree Preservation Orders (TPOs) on any tree, group of trees or woodland (except fruit trees and orchards) which they think are worth protecting, especially ones that would be affected by new building.

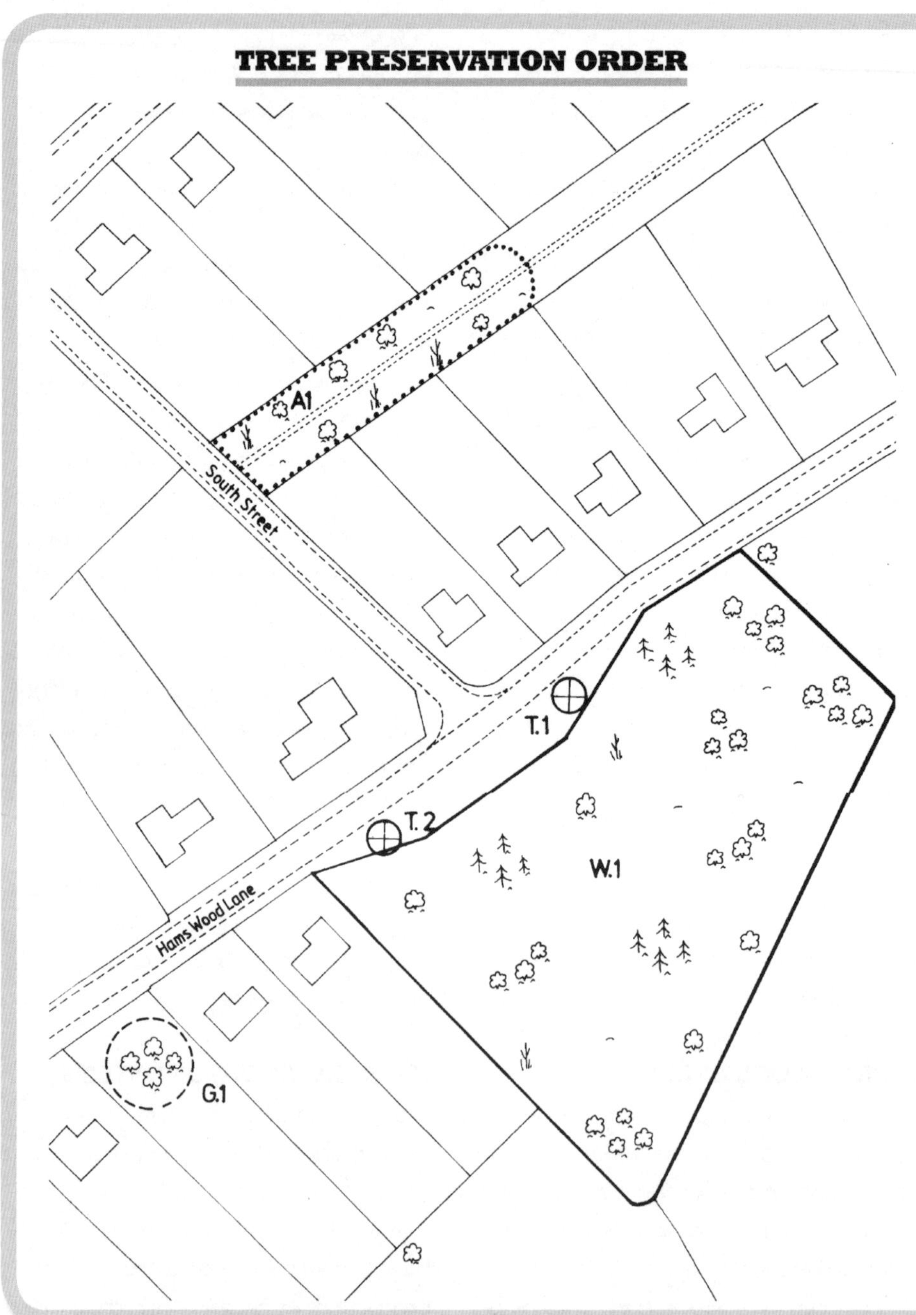

A tree preservation order (TPO) plan shows the areas covered or the individual protected trees:

SCHEDULE

No on map	Description	Situation
Trees specified individually (encircled in black on the map)		
T.1	1 Oak	Land adj Hams Wood Lane, Branchley
T.2	1 Ash	As above
Trees specified by reference to an Area (within a dotted black line on the map)		
A.1	scattered specimens of Ash, Oak, Birch	Area consisting of Land adj South Street
Groups of trees(within a broken black line on the map)		
G.1	6 Oaks	Land adj Hams Wood Lane, Branchley
Woodlands(within a continuous black line on the map)		
W.1	Mixed deciduous woodland comprising: Oak, Ash, Birch, Pine	As above

Figure 12.1

the schedule specifies and describes the trees affected

In practice councils will put TPOs on almost any tree, how ever small, weak, mis-shapen or common, to give themselves greater control over the development of a site when a planning application is made. This raises the dilemma of whether to cut down unprotected trees that would be in the way, before you make a planning application or even speak to a planning officer.

When full planning permission is granted it overrides a TPO and you can fell protected trees to make way for the building. A council is less likely to give permission for a scheme which involves losing trees that it has protected, so your plans should aim to minimise effects on TPO trees. Even if you don't mind an oak tree next to your house, the council will still be worried that the next person to live in the house might. District councils will cheerfully make you reduce your plans for a five-bedroom house to a three-bedroom bungalow in the interests of preserving trees which you've no intention of cutting down in any case. Where trees are protected by a TPO (see Figure 12.1), or where a plot is in a Conservation Area, felling or cutting back trees without going through the proper procedures is against the law. If trees could be a problem on a plot, consult

Figure 12.2

New houses in a Conservation Area matching the proportions and style of the Victorian villas beyond without being replicas

a local arboriculturist who can advise you on the merits of particular trees and the scope for felling, cutting back and replacement.

CONSERVATION AREAS

Conservation Areas are designated by district councils to preserve and enhance the architectural or historic interest of an area. The district council can tell you if a plot is in a Conservation Area and about any special planning policies in the Local Plan or LDF which apply to it. In a Conservation Area, planning applications for new houses are closely scrutinised to make sure that the finished building compliments the area. Special attention is paid to design and materials and the district council could insist on the use of local materials (see Figure 12.2) which can add to your costs. Other implications of being in a Conservation Area are:

Figure 12.3

A side garden plot on a prominent cliff top, adjoining a listed building in a conservation area yet the unpromising circumstances were overcome with a creative design for an underground house

- trees are automatically protected, similar to a TPO
- demolition of buildings needs Conservation Area consent from the district council
- greater restrictions on extensions and alterations that can be built without a planning application
- the possibility of an Article 4 Direction requiring planning applications for external alterations, extensions, outbuildings, etc

If you look at a plot in a Conservation Area, consider whether you would be happy with these constraints. If your plans are for a very distinctive or unusual house with facilities in the garden, such as a swimming pool and tennis court, you should take particular care before buying in a Conservation Area, although contemporary, contrasting or creative designs aren't ruled out by any means (see Figure 12.3).

However, there are benefits to being in a Conservation Area - they're generally attractive and there's less chance of new building ruining the character of the area.

OTHER DESIGNATED AREAS

Other places where there are planning restrictions include Green Belts, National Parks, Areas of Outstanding Natural Beauty or National Scenic Areas, and Sites of Special Scientific Interest. These are shown in Local Plans and LDFs, which also contain particular planning policies that apply to them.

Green Belts are formally designated areas of land around cities, where strict planning policies aim to prevent all but a few limited types of development. The term 'Green Belt' is frequently misused and doesn't mean any open land around all towns and cities. Since planning permission is harder to get in a Green Belt, check the existing permission very carefully. If you hope to demolish and replace an existing building, look up the relevant Local Plan or LDF policies as there could be size restrictions on replacements.

National Parks have their own authorities which deal with planning, drawing up Local Plans/LDFs and deciding planning applications in the park. In National Parks there are fewer permitted development rights to carry out minor building works. If you plan to build in a National Park, and extend the house later, check carefully whether you would get permission.

Areas of Outstanding Natural Beauty (AONBs) and National Scenic Areas (NSAs) in Scotland, are designated to preserve the landscape. Permitted development rights are restricted, the design and materials of new buildings are supposed to reflect local architecture and new buildings have to be sited unobtrusively.

Sites of Special Scientific Interest (SSSIs) protect wildlife and geological features. If your plot is near an SSSI, speak to a planning officer and look in the Local Plan or LDF to find out what restrictions apply.

CHAPTER 13

LEGAL CONSIDERATIONS

Beyond physical and planning points, there are some common legal matters to check. Your solicitors should pick these up but you might be able to spot potential problems early on and it's as well for you to be alert to legal pitfalls.

PLANNING OBLIGATIONS

In order to get planning permission, owners sometimes sign a legal document called a 'planning obligation', also termed a 'planning agreement' or 'section 106 agreement' ('article 40' in Northern Ireland, 'section 75 agreement' in Scotland). This can restrict how land is used, limit what building takes place, make an applicant bear the cost of off-site works needed before building can go ahead or require a financial contribution towards local services or infrastructure. For example, planning obligations could prevent domestic buildings being built on part of the site, require part of the plot to be given to the district council for a public footpath or provide for contributions towards the cost of a new drainage scheme, extra school places or public transport. The requirement for financial contributions in connection with single-house applications is becoming increasingly common and is, in practice, a form of development tax. Council's requirements for contributions, secured by planning obligations, change over time. You could find a new application you make becomes subject to such a payment, which can be substantial, even though one wasn't required for in connection with a previous permission.

Planning obligations are legal charges on the land and so, if you buy a plot subject to a planning obligation, you're bound by its terms. The vendor should tell you about a planning obligation; in any case it'll be in the planning records and noted by your solicitor in his standard pre-purchase searches. Planning obligations can be enforced by district councils and aren't easy to remove. This has to be done by agreement with the council or, with modern ones, after five years you can apply to the council to remove it, with a right of appeal if that's refused. You must show that removal wouldn't harm the area, that the restriction or requirement is obsolete or that a reasonable use of the land is being prevented.

COVENANTS

Requirement to erect a fence

Save to the extent that the property is already fenced the Purchaser hereby covenants to erect and maintain a good and sufficient fence along the boundaries edged in red of a height and style first approved in writing by the Vendor.

Single dwelling only

For the benefit and protection of such part or parts of the land edged blue on the land bound up within as vested in the Vendor at the date of this deed and so as to bind the property into whosoever hands the same may come the Purchaser for himself and his successors in title hereby covenants with the Vendor not to erect upon the property any building other than one private dwelling house with appropriate outbuildings and not to use the same except for occupation as a single private residence.

Figure 13.1

Old covenants can affect whether, where and what you build and new covenants can be imposed when you buy a piece of land

You might come across similar legal agreements, made under the Highways Acts, which require works to a road or access, or a contribution to road improvements,

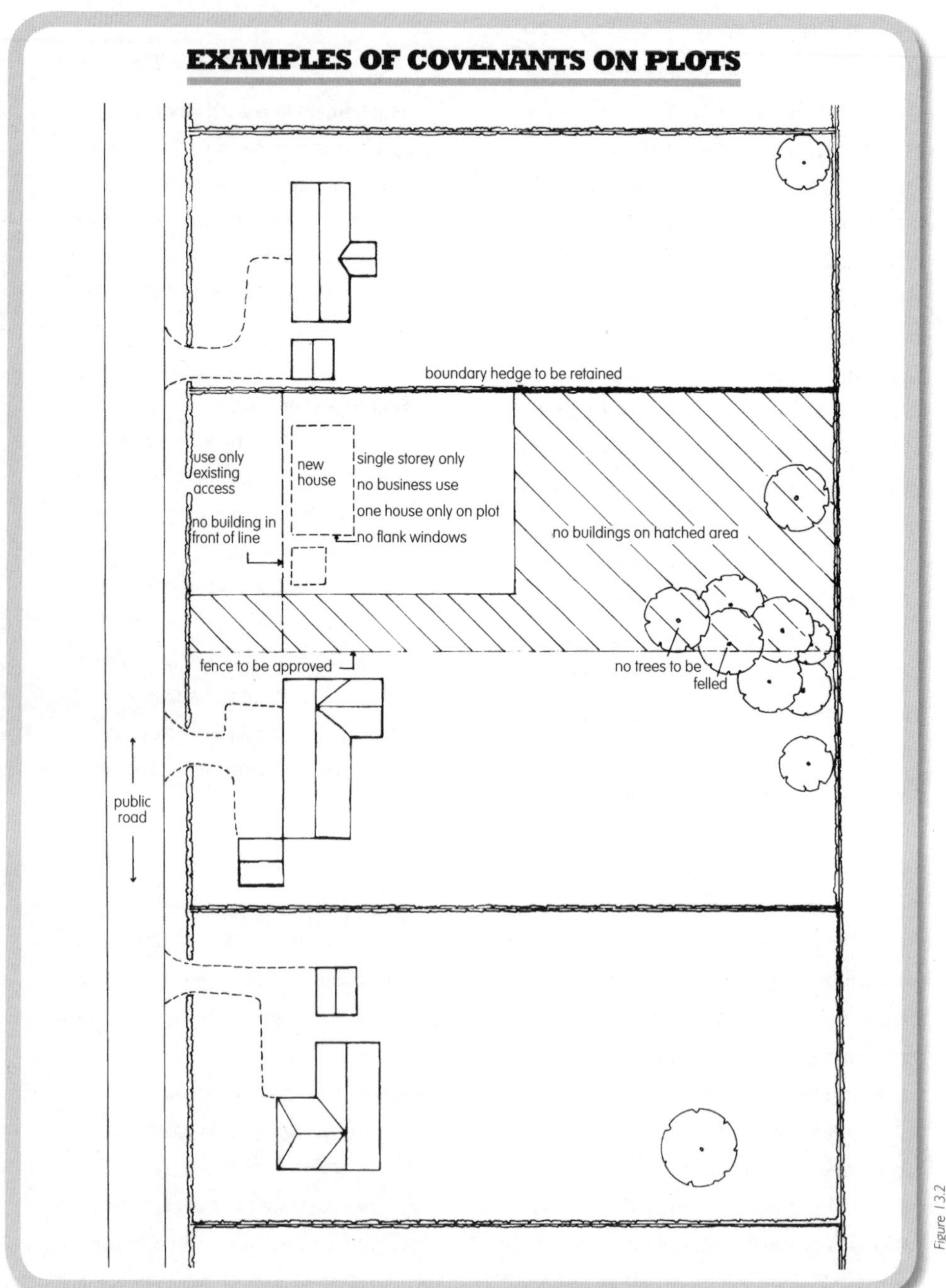

Owners often attach covenants when selling off part of their land to protect the retained property

before building takes place. Planning obligations and highway agreements usually affect the value of a plot and so should be taken into account before you make an offer. You must find out precisely what your obligations would be and have any questions settled by your solicitor.

COVENANTS

A covenant is a binding private agreement between individuals. In Scotland, agreements similar to covenants are known as ancient feus. When buying a plot, purchasers often agree covenants with vendors, for example, to build fences, improve drives, or get vendors' approval of detailed house plans. More important are restrictive covenants that control the way in which a plot is used or developed. They're legally binding and are designed to prevent something from happening on one piece of land, that would otherwise disadvantage another. This is why they often occur where a larger area of land is sub-divided. For example, a large estate might sell off land with restrictive covenants prohibiting houses being built or limiting the height of any houses, to preserve views from the main house. Another common situation where covenants are imposed is when house owners sell-off part of their garden as a plot. To protect the existing house, the owner might state that there can be no commercial use of the new house, specify any trees that must be retained or say that no first-floor windows should overlook the garden of the original house. For examples of what covenants involve, see Figures 13.1 and 13.2.

Planning permission doesn't override restrictive covenants, so even if you get permission to build a two-storey house, a covenant limiting building to single-storey can stop you from carrying out the planning permission. Old restrictive covenants that no longer seem to serve a useful purpose can be troublesome because it might not be clear whether they would or could be enforced. For example, a plot could have a covenant dating from 1910 restricting building but meanwhile a housing estate, supermarket and bypass have separated the plot from the property with the benefit of the covenant. It's difficult to imagine why anybody connected with the original property would be concerned about a building on the plot now, yet a remote possibility remains that the breach of covenant would be noticed. To guard against this, you can take out insurance to cover any claim that might be made. This can be arranged by your solicitor who should advise you on anything to do with covenants.

You can have restrictive covenants removed or relaxed by agreement with the person who has the benefit of the covenant. You're likely to have to pay for this and if the covenant means the difference between building or not, the price will probably be a large proportion of the plot's potential value.

EASEMENTS, WAYLEAVES AND PRIVATE RIGHTS OF WAY

Easements are rights over land such as private rights of way, and rights to maintain pipes and cables. When inspecting a plot, look out for well-trodden footpaths, manhole covers, and cables or pylons as these could point to the existence of easements. Easements for sewers and water mains usually cover a strip of land above and on either side of the pipe. The water company has the right of access to that land for maintenance and also to dig up and replace the pipe but they would have to reinstate your garden. If your plot has pipes or cables running through it, contact the service company concerned to find out the size, depth and age of the pipe and the likelihood of any works being carried out. Ask how any new pipe would be laid, as microtunnelling techniques now avoid the need to dig huge trenches.

Wayleaves are similar to easements and usually the term is used in connection with electricity supply cables where the supply company has a wayleave to carry cables over or under a plot. If pylons or other apparatus are involved, a small annual payment could be made by the supply company for 'rent' of the land involved.

Sometimes there are private rights of way over a plot, either for pedestrians only, or for vehicles as well. These can be diverted or removed by agreement but removal is unlikely if the right of way is the only access to someone else's land. It's possible for rights of way to become established where they've been used unimpeded, over a long period of time, usually at least 20 years. Look for gates and tracks on the plot (see Figure 13.4) and, if somebody claims to have walked across it for the last 30 years and has every intention of continuing to do so, don't dismiss

Figure 13.3

Your solicitor must research ownership and legal restrictions thoroughly before you buy as covenants and ransom strips can prevent building on apparently obvious plots, like this undeveloped village site

the claim out of hand.

Some plots have the benefit of rights over other land. This might simply be a right of access over a private road. Ancient rights over common land still exist in many areas, such as Verderers' rights in the New Forest and Commoners' rights on the Ashdown Forest. Coastal plots can have rights of access to the foreshore. These rights don't usually have cost implications for the owner and are more likely to be selling points for the property. Of course, if you do happen to own a herd of swine, you might find a right to fatten them on acorns from the local wood of some benefit.

FOOTPATHS AND BRIDLEWAYS

Public footpaths and bridleways are usually evident on the ground, may be signposted and are marked on Ordnance Survey maps. Highway authorities keep definitive maps of public rights of way which you

Take note on site of anything that might suggest there could be a public or private right of way and draw it to your solicitor's attention

should inspect if there are any doubts about the existence or route of a path. If a path would hamper building on a plot, you can apply to have it diverted but not until you own the plot. If you want to divert a footpath before buying, the vendor has to apply either on his behalf or on yours. Applications are to the county or district council for a public path diversion order and you'll probably have to pay the council's costs. If the diversion order is opposed, it must be confirmed by the appropriate Secretary of State and compensation is payable to anyone whose rights are harmed by diversion. Discuss the procedure and cost with the appropriate council before applying.

Public rights of way aren't extinguished by the grant of planning permission. So, if you get planning permission to build a house across a footpath, you still need to get a public path diversion order before building works start. The council will have considered the effect on

ASSESSING YOUR PLOT CHECKLIST

Use this checklist as a basis for your assessment of a plot. These factors can affect value, restrict what you can build or stop you building. Don't commit yourself to buying a plot until you have checked each point on the list.

First considerations

Adequate size for house
Lie of the land
Ground conditions
Trees
Obstacles
Orientation
Boundaries
Adjoining uses

Access

Type of road (public/private)
Rights to use private road
Rights of access over other land/ ransom strip
Highway authority standards
Sight lines at access point
Parking and turning space

Services

Method of foul drainage (public/private system)
Method of surface water drainage (public/ soakaway/watercourse)
Rights of access to drains
Water supply
Electricity, gas, telephone
Costs of connection

Planning permission

Type of permission (outline/detailed)
Date of permission
Conditions
Application plans
Planning officer's report
Contact the planning officer

Planning restrictions

Agricultural ties
Article 4 directions
Tree preservation orders (TPOs)
Conservation area
Other designated area

Legal considerations

Planning obligations
Restrictive covenants
Easements, wayleaves and private rights of way
Footpaths and bridleways

the path as part of their normal planning application assessment. Anyone likely to object to diversion of the footpath would probably have objected to the planning application. Finding likely objectors is useful as you might be able to persuade them not to object to the diversion order.

PART 4 VALUING YOUR PLOT

You've found a building plot to buy, it's in the right place and suitable for the house you want to build - but what about the price? Is the asking price reasonable? Is it in line with other plots? How much should you pay? What should you offer? These are the key questions which you face and must find answers to - if you don't want to pay too much or risk losing the plot. You need to know what factors affect values, how to value land and how to work out where to pitch your offer. This Part gives you that information and takes you through the valuation process to making an offer.

CHAPTER 14 FACTORS DETERMINING VALUE

The value of a plot is influenced by a wide range of factors, from the state of the economy through to the nature of the underlying soil. National and local property markets set a general level for plot prices in an area. The value of an individual plot is then determined by what can be built on the site and the cost of the build. We look first at the wider influence on plot values - market conditions.

Plot values are directly related to the housing market - national, regional and local. At the national level, following large falls at the end of the 1980s and early 1990s, land prices rose gradually then sharply into the 2000s, closely following the fortunes of the housing market. Sharp falls in house prices in the late 2000s sent plot prices down again and no doubt the cycle will repeat itself again. National trends can be misleading, however, as they don't reflect wide regional variations, which are especially important if you think of relocating. Find out whether prices are falling or rising in each region, as what's happening in your area, or nationally, might not be happening elsewhere. For example, during the early 1990s property market 'slump', during which building land values fell by 17 per cent in outer London, prices rose by 4 per cent in Northern Ireland and remained stable in Scotland.

As well as differing between regions, prices also vary significantly within each region. Generalisations like, 'property prices in the south-east are the highest in the country' can be misleading. Whilst this might be true of somewhere like Guildford in Surrey, it's certainly not true of, say, Southampton in Hampshire or Gillingham in Kent, where prices are below the national average. There are a number of house price surveys done by building societies like Halifax and Nationwide, and the Land Registry publishes a range of property price information. Use these resources to get an idea of prices in your area but always check local market conditions by talking directly to estate agents and monitoring prices in your area.

Many local factors influence plot prices, including:

- proximity to motorways and main line railway stations
- distance to towns and cities
- local employment prospects
- character of the surrounding countryside
- character of the locality
- availability of building plots
- councils' planning policies

These affect demand and supply and so establish price levels. Most people want to live in places with access to well-paid jobs, schools, leisure and shopping facilities, and in pleasant surroundings. Others are attracted to unspoilt countryside or villages and towns of particular character. Where continuing demand coincides with limited opportunities to build new houses, plot prices will be relatively high. Prices can fluctuate across a county with values higher close to towns and main transport links and lower in the areas in between. There can be spots of higher values where the landscape or scenery is exceptional, or in sought after, picturesque towns and villages. Even within a town or village, there could be an expensive part - perhaps a Conservation Area around the church or green, and a cheaper part - near a factory or railway siding.

Within a local property market, the main factor which indicates a plot's value is the level of prices paid for similar plots in the vicinity.

Figure 14.1

The value of a plot is directly related to the value of the house that can be built on it; finding local house prices in order to value these plots is straightforward here because of similar houses nearby

Sales provide a reference point to establish value and to judge the level of demand. When a plot sells, after a number of offers have been made for it, a comparable plot in the area is likely to attract equal interest and the same sort of price. Remember, the real test is what plots actually sell for, not their asking prices.

All the factors looked at so far determine, generally, the value of a plot. To establish the value of a particular plot, you need to answer three questions:

- what, exactly, can be built on the plot?
- what would it cost to build that building?
- what would be the market value of the finished house?

The answer to the first question is governed by all the points covered in Part Three: physical features, access, services, planning permission, planning restrictions and legal considerations. All except private legal matters are taken into account when a planning application is made and so it's the planning permission that primarily dictates what can be built. This affects value directly - a 0.10 hectare (roughly 0.25 acre) plot with permission for a house of 120 sq m (1,200 sq ft) worth £125,000, could be worth £450,000 with permission for a 300 sq m (3,000 sq ft) house. When you value a plot look carefully at the planning permission but also consider its potential for a larger house, or for more houses, than currently permitted.

The second key question, the cost of the build, depends mainly on the size and type of dwelling and the materials and finishes. You also need to take account of unusual costs associated with a particular site, because of its ground conditions, physical restrictions or legal constraints, for example. You need to answer the third question in order to value a plot, even if you've no intention of selling in the foreseeable future, as the market value of any land is derived from the value of what can be built on it. So the market value of a plot is derived from what the finished house would fetch. The price level of similar houses in the area shows what your house would be worth (see Figure 14.1).

CHAPTER 15 VALUATION METHODS

Valuation isn't a precise science - it's a means of estimating what price a plot would fetch in the market. The simplest form of valuation - and usually the most reliable - is a comparison with other sales. The more sales evidence you have, the better picture you build up of the local plot market and the more accurate your figure. For example, if five plots each with permission for a four-bedroom detached house have sold recently in the same area for £105,000, £96,000, £103,000, £99,000 and £95,500, then you know that the value of a similar plot will be around £100,000. In practice, you don't usually find so many consistent sales so you have to make a comparison between the plot you're valuing and ones that have sold. This is illustrated in the comparable sales table in Figure 15.1. Compare plots in terms of planning permission, size of plot, type of area, setting and physical features. Use house prices to help gauge differences in values between areas. Having made your

VALUING A PLOT USING COMPARABLE SALES

Plot to be valued

0.20 acres (0.08 hectares) with planning permission for a four bedroom chalet in an established residential area

Comparables

Plot	Comments	Sale price (£)
Foxes Lane Thripp	Similar plot but larger. Better position, not on an estate	100,000
Kenmere Walk Thripp	Good comparable. In a residential area. Slightly larger site	90,000
Hall Barn Road Bunting	Planning permission for 3 bed chalet Next to petrol station	70,000
Woodpoke Road Thripp	On country lane. Much larger Next to open countryside with views	130,000
Foxes Lane Thripp	Adjoins woodland. Established garden Has existing access drive	95,000

Valuation
The Foxes Lane plots are in better positions and have advantages over the plot being valued so are more valuable. The Hall Barn Road plot has permission for a smaller house and adjoins a garage so is worth less. Kenmere Walk is most similar to the plot being valued but is slightly larger so is worth slightly more

Value of the plot, therefore £88,000

Figure 10.1

comparison with other plot sales, remember to deduct any unusual costs that wouldn't have been reflected in the prices paid for other plots.

A simple rule-of-thumb method of valuing building plots is used by developers and agents to get an initial idea of value and to see whether an asking price looks reasonable (see Figure 15.2). This involves looking at plot prices as a percentage of the value of the completed house, or its 'resale' value as it's sometimes called. So where a plot sells for £50,000 and the finished house would sell for £200,000, the percentage paid is 25 per cent. Your contacts among

VALUING A PLOT USING 'RULE OF THUMB' METHOD

Plot to be valued

0.20 acres (0.08 hectares) with planning permission for a four bedroom chalet in an established residential area

Sales of other plots

Plot	Estimated value of house (£)	Sale price of plot (£)	Plot price as % of house value
Foxes Lane Thripp	300,000	100,000	33%
Kenmere Walk Thripp	260,000	90,000	35%
Hall Barn Road Bunting	250,000	70,000	28%
Woodpoke Road Thripp	380,000	130,000	34%
Foxes Lane Thripp	270,000	95,000	35%

Average percentage paid for plot = 33%

Estimated value of finished house on plot to be valued	@ rule of thumb %	=	value of plot
£265,000	**@ 33%**	**=**	**£88,000**

Figure 15.2

You can also value of a plot using a percentage of the finished house value or 'rule-of-thumb' method

estate agents involved in plot sales, can give you an idea of the sort of percentages being paid and the approximate value of the house you want to build. For example, if you want to build a three-bedroom chalet bungalow and these are currently selling at around £175,000, and the percentage being paid locally for plots is about 33 per cent, the plot value is going to be around 33 per cent of £175,000, that is, £57,750. There's no set percentage as it varies according to the state of the market and the nature and scarcity of the plot concerned but, typically, the figure is between 25 per cent and 40 per cent. During housing booms percentages of 50 per cent or even more can be paid but the level can slump to below 25 per cent in a depressed housing market. In a rising market, developers assume high sales figures in their calculations to reflect likely price rises during the time it takes to build the house. In a falling market, the opposite is true and developers are pessimistic about the prices they'll get. Unless you believe values will rise or fall significantly in the near future, use current house prices. Don't rely on rule-of-thumb valuations alone unless you can get good local information on the right percentage to use, based on a reasonable volume of recent sales.

The comparable and rule-of-thumb methods of valuation tell you the market value of a plot. There's another method which tells you how much a site is worth, based on your particular scheme - a residual valuation. This is a mathematical calculation of value, starting with an estimate of what the finished house would be worth, then deducting all your build, finance and other costs, to arrive at a residual value for the plot. You can also use the method in reverse to find out if a plot price is reasonable. Take the asking price of the plot, add on the build costs, and see if the total compares with prices of similar houses. An example residual valuation is shown in Figure 15.3. Developers use residual valuations to calculate the maximum amount that they can afford to spend on plots. Their figures have to include full labour costs, profit and overheads. If you're doing some or all of the work yourself or don't need to make a profit, it's up to you whether to include these as costs in your valuation. If you don't, you'll have a higher plot value.

The residual method is useful where your build involves unusual costs or where there aren't enough recent sales on which to base a comparable valuation but it can produce misleading answers if incorrect data are used. In one case we came across, a valuer engaged by a bank produced a detailed residual valuation showing that a plot was worth less than nothing, although the same plot sold a month later for £75,000. Residual valuations are also helpful because they necessitate a detailed examination of the costs and show any potential profit in a scheme. Computer enthusiasts can set up a residual valuation on a spreadsheet and run it making different assumptions about the figures, for example the value of the

VALUING A PLOT USING THE RESIDUAL METHOD

Plot to be valued

0.20 acres (0.08 hectares) with planning permission for a four bedroom chalet in an established residential area

Value of house		**£**
Anticipated value of finished house		265,000
Less agents and legal fees on sale @ 2.5%		6,625
Net proceeds of sale		258,375
Building costs		
Build costs £800/sq m x 140 sq m	112,000	
Garage	10,000	
Access and services	8,000	
Subtotal	130,000	
Contingency (10%)	13,000	
Professional fees	6,000	
Build cost	149,000	
Finance on build		
8% over 12 months ÷ 2	6,000	
Profit @ 10%	15,000	
Total costs		170,000
Balance available for acquiring plot		89,000
Less legal fees on plot purchase		1,000
Balance available to pay for plot		88,000
Value of plot		**88,000**

This valuation assumes a profit level of 10% and selling costs to give a market figure, as commercial builders and developers would allow for such sums in their calculations. This reduces the resulting land value figure but you could reduce or eliminate profit and/or leave out selling costs to arrive at a higher figure in a competitive situation.

Figure 15.3

completed house or the effect of an additional £5,000 of unforeseen expenses. Although many developers use computer programs to produce residual valuations, do use the results with caution and don't lose sight of what the market tells you a plot is worth.

CHAPTER 16

YOUR VALUATION AND OFFER

By the time you've studied agents' particulars and viewed some plots, you'll start to develop a feel for values and for what you can get for your money. If you want to check the value more precisely and make sure that you're paying the right sort of price, carry out your own valuation. In practice, it's best to use all three basic methods of valuation described in the last chapter and compare the figures.

First, try to get as much information as possible on plot sales and prices of houses similar to the one you want to build. This provides the raw data to feed into your valuations. Try to find actual sale prices rather than asking prices. While you're searching for plots, ask estate agents about plots they've sold in the area, how much they sold for and what percentage of the finished house price this represented. Find out at the same time who's buying plots - individuals or builders/developers - as this could influence the offer you make later. Agents are reluctant to give precise figures on sales, especially where sales haven't yet been completed. They might say whether the asking price was exceeded or whether the price went over, say, £100,000, which would give you an idea of the price paid. Auction results give a good indication of market value and, because they're held in public, the agent is more likely to tell you the result and auction results are published. Keep a note of anything you learn, to use in your calculations - the more local and recent the information, the more accurate your valuation will be.

Find out house prices from estate agents' websites, adverts in local newspapers and in estate agents' windows. Where you buy a plot through agents, ask them to put a figure on the house you intend to build. Tell them precisely the size and style of house and show them any drawings, so they can then give you a more specific price. If you're on good terms with other estate agents, try asking them for a figure as well. Generally agents are willing to do this as they hope to get the eventual sale of the house.

Once you've done your market research, carry out your valuations. Where you can find out about recent sales of similar plots, market value is best gauged by comparing your plot with those sales. Do this exactly as described in the previous chapter. Note the location and appearance of the other plots in order to make a proper comparison with yours. Making adjustments to reflect any differences between plots isn't scientific but depends on sensible judgements. Information about one sale of a near identical plot is a better basis for valuation than of any number where there are significant differences. Use all the available information to reach a figure.

A rule-of-thumb percentage valuation is very straightforward, where there's a good indication of what percentage of house prices is being paid for plots. Apply this to the value of your house when finished, to arrive at a figure for the plot.

A residual valuation takes time to carry out but it's worthwhile because it gives you a land price based on your own project and shows whether your project is financially sound. The budget prepared before you started looking for a plot indicates approximately the maximum amount of money you have available to buy a site. You can use much of the information in your budget to do a residual valuation.

Get more detailed figures on building costs and finance, if you need them, from your self-build package company or building designer and from your bank or building society. Use the example residual valuation given in the last chapter as a guide (see Figure 15.3). Decide whether you want to include profit and full labour and finance costs in your calculation. Builders and developers have to include these costs but individuals don't and this can be reflected in the amount they're prepared to offer for a plot.

A potential cost to keep in mind when considering value is the payment of any financial contributions under a planning obligation (see Chapter 13). Where such costs are present, they should be reflected in the price paid for the land or, when carrying out comparable valuation, make sure you know whether other sites were subject to similar payments. Where you would be making a new detailed planning application, check with the council whether its requirements for or levels of contributions have changed or might change before you would be likely to submit your application.

Valuing a plot is more complicated where development potential is involved. A plot with planning permission for a modest house might be able to take a much larger house - there might be planning permission for one house but enough space for two. The extent to which any potential should be reflected in the price you pay depends on the likelihood of getting planning permission. To value potential, work out what the plot would be worth if an improved planning permission was given and compare that figure with what the plot is worth with its existing permission. The difference between these is the maximum additional value that could possibly be realised and a proportion of this can be reflected in the price. The right proportion depends on the chances of getting planning permission and is usually anything up to about two-thirds. So, if the current value of a plot is £130,000 but, with a new permission, would be £160,000 and the prospects for a new permission are good, you might decide the potential is worth £10,000 (160,000 - 130,000 = 30,000 x say 33 per cent = £10,000). Unless there's a realistic prospect of getting planning permission, ignore development potential in your figures. Vendors naturally tend to overstate potential and the only way to put this beyond doubt is to make a planning application but, if permission were actually to be obtained, the vendor would then want to be paid the full value.

Where potential is involved, or where the valuation of a plot is complex, consider taking professional advice, ideally from a locally-based firm of Chartered Surveyors or valuers which is involved in the building plot market. Advice can vary from an opinion of value through to a formal report and valuation. If you've done some of the ground-work yourself, for example, finding out about comparable sales, give the information to the valuer as it might save him time and you money. In a complex case you might pay several hundred pounds for a formal valuation but, if this saves you several thousand pounds, it's money well spent.

So far we've looked at how to calculate the market value of a plot objectively. Remember that, in doing a valuation, you're making an estimate of what a site will fetch. No matter what sum your calculations produce, a piece of land is ultimately worth what someone is prepared to pay for it.

There are other factors which you might need to take into account when it actually comes to making an offer. Each plot you look at inevitably has an element of value personal to you, reflecting your own preferences and circumstances. You might attach personal value to: locations near family, workplace or existing house; a view; established gardens; being close to open countryside; or being able to buy quickly or at a certain time. None of these things can be valued objectively - it's for you to judge how much they're worth.

Although you shouldn't lay too much weight on the vendor's asking price, it's still a factor which you need to take into account in working out what offer to make. If no asking price is quoted, ask the selling agent what he thinks the vendor would accept. Asking prices aren't usually too far from the market value, although there are always exceptions. Some vendors try it on by asking unreasonably high figures but this shouldn't stop you making a lower offer. In a rising market asking prices are often exceeded by prices actually paid and in a falling market vendors often have to take less than the asking price. In Scotland, asking prices are set low and offers are invited above the figure given.

Sometimes a plot is put on the market at what appears to be well below market value. You might have stumbled upon a vendor who is desperate, wants a very quick sale, or has been badly advised. More likely, the low price reflects a problem like a covenant, a ransom strip, an inconvenient right of way across the land or unstable ground conditions. Ask the vendor or his agent whether the site has any problems and, if nothing is apparent on the ground, warn your solicitor of this if a sale goes ahead.

In talking to the vendor or his agent, try to find out whether other people are interested in the plot and whether they're likely to make offers. If you're the only person interested in a particular plot, you might be able to buy it for far less than its theoretical value. On the other hand, another keen purchaser might be willing to pay well over the general market value. You need to reflect the level and strength of competition in your figure.

Before you put forward an offer you should have formed a view on the market value, calculated what you can afford to pay and decided what the plot is worth to you. You should also have an idea of the vendor's expectations - either a price, or at least an indication of the sort of figure that would be accepted. The right level for your offer depends on the state of the market, the likelihood of other competing bids, and how much you want that particular plot. Professional advice can help you to an extent but, ultimately, the decision on how much to pay for a plot rests with you.

VALUING YOUR PLOT CHECK LIST

- Find out the asking price
- Look for information on comparable plot sales
- Find out the level of house prices and estimate what your finished house will be worth
- Carry out comparable, rule-of-thumb and residual valuations
- Consider whether to get a professional valuation
- Decide how much to offer based on your valuations and taking account or personal factors, market competition and the vendor's expectation

PART 5 BUYING YOUR PLOT

Plots are sold in different ways and each method has its opportunities and pitfalls. There are tactics which you can use in putting forward offers and negotiating, to secure your purchase successfully. Competition for plots can be fierce and, unless you know what goes on behind the scenes, you could well be unsuccessful. This Part guides you through the steps involved in buying your plot and highlights the action that you should take.

CHAPTER 17
BUYING LAND

Most building plots are sold by private treaty, exactly as houses are bought and sold. In this chapter, we look at the main parties involved in a purchase, and follow the private treaty procedure through to completing a purchase.

KEY PLAYERS

The key players in the purchase of a building plot are:

- the vendor
- the vendor's agent
- you, the purchaser
- the two parties' solicitors or licensed conveyancers
- any competing buyers

Vendors may be private individuals, companies, local authorities, trusts, organisations, in fact almost anybody. Most plots are sold by private individuals, builders and developers and, in some areas, by local authorities. Their willingness to negotiate, supply information, act quickly, and co-operate generally varies, although most recognise that it's in their interests to help you as much as possible.

Vendors' agents differ enormously in their approach to the task of selling a plot. Some remain behind their desks and do nothing much to help, saying that it's for you to satisfy yourself about planning, drainage, services and all other points. Others will be found crashing about in the brambles, banging in site boundary markers, peering into drains and measuring sight lines at the access. They might give you copies of planning documents, letters from service companies and details of the size and depth of the nearest sewer. Whichever camp the agents fall in, make sure they recognise that you're a serious buyer. Don't forget that they're not working for you but for the vendor. However, if helping you speeds the arrival of their commission cheque, you can expect some degree of service from them. Don't hesitate to ask agents questions but always check the answers for yourself. This applies especially to anything that could affect the cost or your ability to build the house you want on the plot.

Anybody can be an estate agent and sell building plots, regardless of qualifications. Those with professional training will be members of the Royal Institution of Chartered Surveyors (RICS) or the National Association of Estate Agents (NAEA). You can expect a professional approach from members of these organisations, even though membership doesn't guarantee knowledge or experience of selling development land. If an agent, qualified or not, seems to have no idea what he's talking about or is unhelpful, try talking directly to the vendor.

Solicitors and conveyancers too have different levels of knowledge and experience with building plots. Most deal with buying and selling plots from their desks - a practical necessity if they're based 200 miles from the site. Stay in touch with your solicitor throughout your purchase but don't try to contact the vendor's solicitor – he's unlikely to speak to you, as solicitors don't like short-circuiting long-winded lines of communication.

Competing buyers are always a threat to your purchase, right up to exchange of contracts. Some could be professional developers with knowledge of planning, much experience of buying plots and armed with sophisticated computer programmes to check their valuations. They also hold an ace card with which to woo the estate agent - the finished house to sell - earning the agent a second commission from the same piece of land. Don't be put off. Developers, builders, speculators and investors have to make a profit after staff have been paid and the finished house marketed, advertised and sold. This gives you an ace card too - the ability to outbid the developer. Other individuals might be after the same plot as you. If you're better prepared and ready to move quickly, you can snap it up before they've put together their offer. Detailed and accurate budgeting could give you the confidence to offer that extra £500 needed to secure the plot, without risking your scheme's viability.

PRIVATE TREATY SALES

In England, Wales and Northern Ireland, most plots are sold by private treaty. In Scotland some sales are conducted by private treaty, however, the majority take place through a different system, where sealed bids are submitted and the deal becomes binding on acceptance of a bid. As this is a type of tender, the system in Scotland is examined in Chapter 20. There are three distinct stages in a purchase by private treaty:

- negotiations prior to an offer being accepted
- accepting an offer to exchange of contracts
- exchange of contracts to completion of the purchase

The chart in Figure 17.2 shows the private treaty procedure, explaining what buyers and their solicitors do at the different stages of a transaction. Procedure varies slightly depending on whether the title of the plot is registered. There's nothing terribly complicated about private treaty sales procedure, although legal documents aren't always easy to understand, being littered with obscure language and entirely lacking in any form of punctuation. It's technically possible for you to do your own conveyancing but this isn't a good idea for a plot purchase. If you build your own home, you'll be saving money, so invest a small part of this in a good solicitor or licensed conveyancer - it's money well spent.

The first stage of the purchase is negotiation, which comprises everything that happens before an offer is accepted by the vendor. During this time you might make all the right moves but you've no control over the outcome. It's only when your offer is accepted by the vendor that you start to move towards a formal agreement to buy. Negotiations are usually carried out 'subject to contract' which means that nothing agreed is legally binding until contracts are exchanged, preventing you being caught out, if a problem with the plot comes to light, after an offer has been accepted but before exchange of contracts. Letters concerning sales are often still marked 'subject to contract', although this isn't legally necessary.

When your offer is accepted, the vendor's agent usually draws up a memorandum of sale. This isn't a legal document and merely sets out what's been agreed, the names of the vendor and purchaser and their solicitors. It could be a formal-looking document, as in the example (see Figure 17.3), or simply a letter. It's normally sent to all the people listed on it, together with a copy of the sales particulars. If there's no agent involved, inform your solicitors and give them the name of the vendor's solicitors. Offer and acceptance should be confirmed in writing to avoid misunderstandings.

Once your offer has been accepted, the solicitors or conveyancers will set to work. Before exchange of contracts your solicitor carries out searches and sends enquiries about the property to the vendor's solicitor. The searches involve inspecting the local land charges register and sending a list of standard questions to the district council. Any covenants or easements should come to light at this stage, plus information on any major development or road schemes that affect the site. Information you get about proposed or likely development is very limited in standard searches and so you could consider commissioning a planning consultant separately to research planning permissions and potential of nearby land. In addition to the solicitor's normal searches, and before contracts are exchanged, you should check:

- that planning permission will be given for exactly what you want to build
- that all service and drainage connections can be made (and the costs involved)
- if ground conditions are poor, the cost of special foundations
- that the precise boundaries of the site are clear and match the title plan
- that finance arrangements are agreed and the bank or building society's solicitor is instructed to deal with any new mortgage

Figure 17.1

When you see a plot for sale be ready to move quickly; contact the estate agents to let them know you're interested and stay in touch with them throughout the purchase

Remember that once contracts are exchanged, you can't pull out of your purchase without paying a penalty.

Make certain that the sale plans, the site boundaries, and what you believe you're buying, are all one and the same. Boundary disputes often occur when land is sold, either between vendor and purchaser or between a new owner and neighbours. To avoid disputes, get a plan showing measured boundaries that are pegged out on site and agreed by all parties. The best way to do this is to meet the vendor or his agent on site, agree and mark out boundaries with wooden posts banged well in to the ground, and then take measurements. This is particularly important where, for example, a vendor is selling part of his garden. Having agreed what to sell, the vendor could realise that he's losing a treasured tree and decide to redefine the boundary.

This must be thrashed out before contracts are exchanged and could hold up the sale.

You normally pay a deposit on exchange of contracts, usually 10 per cent of the agreed price, which isn't repayable if you fail to complete the purchase. The completion date is fixed at exchange of contracts and is usually two to four weeks after exchange, although anything from two days to two months wouldn't be uncommon. Between exchange of contracts and completion, the solicitors complete the formalities and arrange for the money to be transferred. Where you take out a mortgage to buy the plot, your solicitor liaises with the bank or building society. The time between exchange and completion gives you the chance to finalise plans, deal with planning permission or to get ready to start building. Whether to make any commitments during this period, such as ordering a kit house, is for you and your solicitor to decide. The plot only becomes yours after completion. Before that, there's always a risk that the sale might not go through. You can sue a vendor for breach of contract and claim any losses you incur but this is time-consuming, costly and fruitless if he doesn't have any money. To be safe, don't commit any significant amounts of money to your project, prior to completion, without consulting your solicitor first.

CONTRACTS

The most common type of contract is one that simply records the sale of a plot by one party to another subject, of course, to payment. This is known as an outright purchase and from a vendor's point of view is usually the best way to sell a plot. However, a purchaser might be prepared to buy a plot but be unwilling to do so unless some other matter is resolved first, like a grant of planning permission. In these circumstances, a conditional contract is often a useful way forward. Conditional contracts are typically used where:

- there's outline planning permission but the buyer wants detailed permission before finally committing himself
- the buyer wants a different planning permission
- planning permission hasn't been given and the vendor is unwilling or unable to spend money to get it
- a legal matter needs to be resolved, such as a right of way to be negotiated or a restrictive covenant to be overcome

PRIVATE TREATY SALE PROCEDURE

YOU	SOLICITOR
OFFER *Make an offer to the vendor, negotiate, agree a price, your offer is accepted.*	
INSTRUCT SOLICITOR *Tell your solicitor a sale has been agreed, give the names and addresses of the vendor, agent and solicitor, and your lender.*	**INITIAL WORK** *Make enquiries and asks for contract and title documents from vendor's solicitor, carries out searches, contacts your lender.*
CONTRACT *Read report and sign contract, give dates for exchange and completion, supply cheque for deposit.*	**REPORT** *Reports to you: ownership, replies to enquiries, results of searches, and contract.*
	EXCHANGE *Date agreed for completion, contracts exchanged, lender notified, prepares conveyance.*
PURCHASE MONEY *You or your lender provide money for balance of purchase price.*	**COMPLETION** *Pays over money in return for ownership documents.*
POSSESSION *The plot becomes yours and you take over responsibility for it, pay solicitor.*	**REGISTRATION** *Pays stamp duty and registers the land in your name with HM Land Registry.*

Figure 17.2

MEMORANDUM OF SALE

Re: the proposed sale of: Plot adjoining 22 Highfield Avenue, Trant

SUBJECT TO CONTRACT

Vendor:	JB Builders Ltd, The Forge, High Street, Trant
Solicitor:	Finch, Wilson and Co, 47 East Row, Bantley For the attention of Mr C Nyman
Purchaser:	Mr and Mrs H Longford, 87 Harding Road, Copton
Solicitor:	Beason Birch, 32 High Street, Songton For the attention of Ms J West
Price agreed:	£90,000 (ninety thousand pounds) subject to contract
Deposit held:	N/A
Tenure:	Freehold
Finance/Mortgage:	N/A
Local Authority:	Trant Borough Council, Town Hall, North Road, Trant

Remarks and Special Conditions:
The Purchaser will be responsible for fencing the plot, details to be approved by the Vendor

A copy of this memorandum has been sent to both parties and their respective Solicitors.

Signed on behalf of
Hallingtons, Estate Agents:

B Metcalfe

B J Metcalfe MRICS
Date: 26th September 2009

Figure 17.3

A memorandum of sale records the parties, property and price agreed

■ there's a physical obstacle to overcome, such as the means of drainage to be resolved or sight lines to be improved at the access

The purpose of the conditional contract is to give you security while you spend time and money on the plot or work on a problem that has to be resolved. Strictly speaking, what's often called a conditional contract is actually a contract subject to conditions. Leave these legal niceties to your solicitor. The important point here is that you should have a contract, albeit with conditions attached, and not a non-binding agreement to enter a contract if certain conditions are fulfilled. The latter is a conditional offer and you could result in you spending hundreds of pounds getting planning permission only for the vendor to sell to someone else. Your solicitor deals with the detail of a conditional contract. Where a contract is made conditional on planning permission, there are important points to check:

■ is the contract subject to you obtaining full or outline planning permission?

■ if permission is granted subject to planning conditions, what planning conditions would be unacceptable?

■ if the council resolves to grant planning permission subject to a legal agreement, what terms or requirements in such an agreement would be unacceptable?

■ if planning permission is refused, does the contract allow for an appeal?

■ if an appeal is dismissed, does the contract allow for the submission of a new scheme?

■ does the contract take account of the period during which a permission could be the subject of a legal challenge?

■ where the vendor has a mortgage, does he have the permission of the building society to enter into the contract?

You and your solicitor must consider these possibilities carefully to avoid becoming committed to buy a plot when planning permission is given, only to find that you're unable to build the house you want because of some defect in the permission.

So far, we've looked at conditional contracts from a buyer's point of view, however, these contracts must be negotiated with the vendor. He probably wants a quick completion and might not be willing to wait while you indulge in lengthy planning battles over some design feature of your dream house that has little bearing on the plot value. The vendor could try to restrict the time allowed to get your permission and insist on a cut-off date to stop matters dragging on, after which the contract ends. Remember that the whole purpose of the conditional contract is to give you time to sort out planning or other matters. Allow at least five months to gain planning permission; if the vendor won't give you adequate time, don't enter into the contract.

An alternative to a conditional contract is an option to buy a plot which, as the name suggests, is a legal right to buy a property at some future date. Options are widely used by developers who buy an option on a piece of land with potential and then try to get planning permission on it. An option involves paying a sum now – which might be nominal - for the right to buy within a certain number of years, either for a fixed amount or for a percentage of the open market value when the option is exercised and the land acquired. This is a way to stop others buying a plot while you work on it or decide whether to go ahead and buy it. To a landowner, an option can be attractive as it involves receiving some immediate cash while someone else works to make his land more valuable. Consider an option where:

- you find a perfect site but aren't in a position to buy straight away
- you're not sure that you can get planning permission for the house you want to build
- you want to secure one or more sites for future projects

What you pay for an option, and then for the plot itself, is a matter for negotiation and agreement between the parties. The level depends on a number of factors including the amount of down payment at the start, the degree of risk, the amount of work to be shouldered by the purchaser and whether anyone else is interested in the plot. With the purchase of a single plot, a fixed figure is usually agreed but, if you did agree to pay a percentage of the full market value with planning permission, this would normally be in the region of 70-85 per cent. You must pay something for the option, even if it's just £1, otherwise it won't be legally binding. Take advice from your solicitor on whether a conditional contract or option is most suitable for the circumstances of your purchase. The main advantage of an option is that you don't have to proceed to buy if you don't want to. If you do consider trying to secure an option on a plot, discuss it with your solicitor who'll need to draft a suitable option agreement. Key points to be covered are:

- the sum to be paid
- the duration of the option
- the steps to be taken to obtain planning permission
- the price to be paid for the land or how it's to be calculated
- provisions in the case of disputes

PURCHASE AND TAKING POSSESSION

After exchange of contracts, the purchase is in the hands of your solicitor or conveyancer and progress to completion should be a formality. However, things can go wrong even at this late stage. Your solicitor could still find defects in the vendor's ownership - for example, part of the access could turn out to be in private ownership and not part of the adopted highway or a registered title incorrectly registered. Ask your solicitor to keep you informed, especially of problems that arise. Don't accept legal jargon - get explanations in terms that you understand. Ask about the implications of any problems and how long they'll take to resolve. Where questions of ownership arise that could affect your ability to build on the plot, resolve them prior to completion. If a query about, say, the exact position of a rear boundary doesn't fundamentally affect your plans for the plot, proceed with the purchase but don't do this unless your solicitor has clearly explained any risks involved.

Occasionally a buyer is unable to complete the purchase and has to default on the contract. You risk not only losing your deposit but also risk further claims from the vendor. Again, discuss any difficulties you have with your solicitor.

Completion of the purchase allows you to take possession of the plot. If you think security could be a problem, arrange for some form of fencing on completion day or before you store materials on the plot. As soon as you purchase a plot you need to take out public liability insurance because, for example, if your soil engineer were to dig a hole to test ground conditions and a trespasser fell in and was injured, you'd be liable.

When you take possession, you're limited in what you can do without planning permission. If you already have detailed planning permission and building regulations approval, you can go ahead and build, as long as any conditions requiring approval of the council prior to commencement of the works have been discharged. If you don't have planning permission or only have an outline permission, you shouldn't start work. If you do, you might upset the council and neighbours, which might not help your cause when you make a detailed planning application. Having planning permission to build a new home doesn't automatically mean that you can live in a caravan or mobile home on the plot, although this is something of a grey area in planning. The basic rule is that you need separate permission to live in a caravan or mobile home on the plot, unless you're fully employed in the construction of the house. Councils have stopped people living in caravans on site where:

- a self-builder, because of injury, had to bring in sub-contractors to complete the building
- an owner travelled to his plot every weekend to build a retirement home; because he had a full-time job elsewhere, he was not 'employed', in building the house
- a family converting a barn stopped building for financial reasons and were not then 'employed' on the building as no work was taking place

This doesn't mean you have to lay every brick yourself and you can satisfy the tests by having a managerial role in the building. If you're not going to be fully employed in the building of your home, you can speak to a planning officer at the district council about living in a caravan on site. In practice, it's unlikely that the council would be concerned about the temporary siting of a caravan. Even if it was, the chances are that you would have finished building and moved into the house before the council came to take action to remove the caravan.

CHAPTER 18

MAKING AN OFFER AND NEGOTIATION

In areas and times of high demand, good plots can attract a dozen or more firm offers. The buyers who succeed are well prepared, act quickly and read the state of the market accurately to outbid their rivals. We saw earlier how to assess and value a plot. During the course of that process you'll probably have spoken to the vendor's agents; if not, contact them as soon as you think a particular plot is right for you. Say that you're about to make an offer, that your finance is in place and that your solicitor is geared up for an early exchange of contracts. Ideally, have a letter from your lender or bank confirming that funds are available. Ask about other interested buyers and whether any offers have been made, at what level, and when a decision is likely. Find out how the agents intend to proceed and whether there would be an opportunity to review your offer if there are other offers at the same or a higher level.

Make your offer as soon as you

LETTER MAKING AN OFFER ON A PLOT

Bob and Sue Fosdyke
42 Nelson Avenue
Fairnborough
Hunts
FC6 5FT

12th January 2009

Snetterton Chapstick Estate Agents
41 The Chase
Stollington
Hunts
FC3 3ES

For the attention of Yasmin de Silva

Dear Sir

PLOT AT GRAFTONS, WISSLE CRESCENT, STOLLINGTON

I refer to my recent phone conversation with Mrs de Silva and now confirm our offer for this property of £90,000 (ninety thousand pounds).

I enclose a copy of a letter from my lender confirming the availability of funds for the purchase.

My solicitor is Mr Jeremy Sneed of Plumper Sneed, 22 The Chase, Stollington FC3 3ET.

If this offer is accepted, my solicitor will respond quickly to receipt of a draft contract, with a view to an early exchange and completion.

Yours faithfully

B Fosdyke

Bob Fosdyke

Figure 18.1

A letter making an offer for a property doesn't have to observe any formalities but it's a good idea to confirm the essential ingredients of your bid: the amount, the availability of funds and the intention to go ahead without delay – all music to a vendor's and agent's ears have all your information to hand but don't recklessly throw in a figure with a view to adjusting it later, as this wouldn't impress the agents or vendor and, ultimately, could spoil your chances. If you're still waiting for information which is delaying your offer, tell the vendor's agents. Provided you convince them that you're a serious buyer, they're likely to advise the vendor to delay a decision until your offer is in.

Judging the right level for your offer isn't usually difficult if, during your plot-finding and valuing, you gain a clear picture of the local plot market using the valuation methods suggested earlier (see Chapter 15). You should know the asking price, market value, what you would like to pay and what is the most you could pay. In a busy market, don't try to get away with too low a figure. If several offers are made and yours is one of the lowest, you might not get a chance to increase your figure. In a slow market, and particularly if there's little, or no, competition, start with a low offer, especially if the plot's been on the market for any length of time. Look at the chances of finding another plot if you fail to buy this one and think about whether this plot is right and you really want to buy it. Ultimately, only you can balance all the factors and make the decision.

Making an offer is a simple process - telephone the vendor's agents and tell them what figure you're offering and that you'll confirm it in writing. They're likely to ask whether you've a house to sell, who your lender is, what you intend to build and who your solicitor is. Include these details in your letter, as shown in Figure 18.1. Don't make your offer subject to any other, for example '£500 more than the highest'; this would be extremely reckless. Your offer should clearly state if it's conditional - dependent on planning permission for example - or whether you want to enter into a conditional contract.

Developers sometimes include uplift clauses in offers, allowing for an additional amount to be paid if they get a better planning permission or a higher price than expected when they come to sell the finished house. These clauses make offers more attractive to vendors but, unless you intend to sell quickly, an uplift clause based on a sale price isn't appropriate. Uplift clauses are written into contracts and would need to be discussed with your solicitor.

NEGOTIATING

Once an offer is made it may be accepted outright, although sometimes there's a period of negotiation due to competing offers or because your offer simply falls below the vendor's expectations. In the latter case the agent usually knows the figure at which the vendor would sell and might tell you the figure or ask you to increase your offer. If yours is the only offer, you're in a strong position but the vendor might begin a further round of advertising and marketing to drum up a better figure. However, the agents won't relish this prospect as it'll mean more work for the same commission. If your figures allow for an increase and the price still appears to be at a reasonable market level, by all means make a revised offer. Sound out the agents carefully before you do this and, if you sense that the vendor is in a hurry to sell, try adding the incentive of a fast exchange of contracts and completion to your original offer. Make sure your solicitor knows what you're offering - if he's just about to start his annual holiday, you could have problems delivering your extra-quick purchase.

Where there are competing offers, the sale might go a number of different ways. Agents monitor the level of interest in a plot, record who offers what and when, and report regularly to their client, the vendor. The sample diary extract in Figure 18.2 shows how agents might record the offers received on a plot. Where more than one offer is made, they must decide which to advise their client to accept. The vendor is interested primarily in the amount of money and the certainty of the buyer completing the sale. You must make sure that the agent has confidence in your ability to go ahead. You'll probably meet the agent once or twice or possibly only speak to him on the telephone. From these fleeting communications, the agent will sum you up. This isn't a sophisticated process: you'll be seen as either a genuine purchaser or a time-waster. Those in the latter category face an uphill struggle in any negotiations and risk being excluded altogether. The secret in dealing with agents is to be well-prepared and businesslike, as this gives the right message. If your message is that you're thinking about building your own

ESTATE AGENTS FILE NOTES ON A PLOT SALE

Property	PINT POT LANE
Client	MR & MRS DOPPLEGATE
21/02/09	Clients confirm instructions to market plot and approve particulars. Sale board arranged, advert placed
01/03/09	Phone call from Mr Misker, 14 Swinbourne Avenue, Handle 01654 778321, offer £80,000, has house to sell so is not ready to go ahead with purchase immediately
03/03/09	Jason Snippet, Marlpitt Developments called into the office, offer £80,000 with early exchange of contracts, confirmed he would give us re-sale of finished house
03/03/09	Mrs A Pincham emailed offer of £79,000 and gave financial references, her solicitors are Bentwhistle & Co, can buy quickly
10/03/09	Phone call from Jason Snippet asking if his offer is OK, arranged to meet Jason for lunch next Friday
15/03/09	Phone call from Raymond Porks, Rocks House, Brinkley 01861 439117, tentative offer of £73,000, he is still talking to planning officers about the plot and hopes to have finances in place by next week so he can confirm his offer, sounds a bit vague
18/03/09	Phone call to clients recommending they accept Marlpitt Development's offer as the highest and the company is reliable. Clients want to us to ask for best and final offers. Recommend we leave out Mr Misker as he has a property to sell and Raymond Porks as he has not made a firm offer. Agree to seek best and final offers from Marlpitt Developments and Mrs Pincham by 25th. Notify Misker and Porks they have been unsuccessful
23/03/09	Phone call from Jason Snippet, he will increase his offer, fishing for clues on what price would get him the plot
25/03/09	Written offers made, Mrs Pincham £88,000 with early exchange, Jason Snippet £85,000 with early exchange. Phone clients, both offers look certain, clients want to take highest offer. Put sale in hand, memorandum of sale completed and sent Jason Snippet notified he was not successful

Figure 18.2

These agent's file notes show how he might react to offers being made for a plot. Approaches will vary but, in this case, with a little prompting from his client, the agent has got it right. Mrs Pincham was lucky to get the plot as she nearly lost it to the developer by making a low initial offer. The developer made the right moves but, when it came to best and final offers, couldn't top the private purchaser. Mr Misker made an offer at the right level but, without finance ready, his offer wasn't sound. Mr Porks' figure was too low and too vague home one day but haven't thought much about it, you're giving the wrong signals.

Once you make an offer for a plot, there's an uncertain stage before it's accepted, lasting hours or weeks. Negotiations can be complex, especially when a number of people all want the same plot and events can take a number of courses:

- there's a clear winner whose offer is accepted
- the offers are close and all bidders, or the top two or three, are invited to make revised offers
- an informal tender is held, where best and final offers are invited by a certain date
- a Dutch auction is held
- a contracts race takes place

Where you're invited to reconsider your offer, you must decide how badly you want the plot and how close to your maximum figure you're prepared to go. Everyone likes a bargain but, where there's competition, it might take your best offer to secure the plot. Get as much information as you can from the agents about other offers and the vendor's expectations. Agents vary in helpfulness but try asking their advice on the right level to offer. Judge their comments against your knowledge of the plot market and don't be tempted to go over your maximum figure.

INFORMAL TENDERS

Informal tenders are held where there are several offers but no obvious winner has emerged. This could follow the first round of offers or be used after revised offers have been made. The agents invite buyers to make their best and final offers, in writing, by a given time and date. The tender is described as 'informal' because the vendor doesn't have to accept the highest, or any, offer and acceptance doesn't immediately create a binding contract. From a purchaser's point of view, an informal tender is something of a shot in the dark - it's your best offer against other people's. You must simply go in as high as you can, bearing in mind your budget. Find out as much as you can about the competition. Developers, builders and speculators make offers that aren't too far from market value. Private individuals are less predictable. If the plot is exceptional in some way, offers are sometimes made well above the theoretical value of the plot.

Send your written offer in

response to an informal tender to the agents in good time before the close of the tender period and check that it's arrived. If you're unhappy with the way the sale is being handled or are suspicious about the relationship between other buyers and the agents, deliver your offer personally just before the time when the tender closes. Sometimes agents provide a form and envelope for your tender; if not, clearly mark the outside of the envelope, otherwise it could be opened accidentally before the proper time. Make sure that your tender gives all the information required by the agents, which might include the name and address of your solicitor or conveyancer and possibly a financial reference. Even if these aren't asked for, there's nothing to lose in supplying them anyway. Sometimes offers are made of a sum like £50,001, in the hope of beating another's of £50,000, but it's generally better to work in units of at least £100.

Once an informal tender has been held it's highly unlikely that any further negotiation will take place. The successful bidder is informed and a memorandum of sale is drawn up and the sale goes ahead.

DUTCH AUCTIONS

'Dutch auction' is the name usually given to what is actually a private auction. Bidders are told the highest bid and invited to bid against each other. A real Dutch auction is actually an auction where the price starts high and falls slowly until a buyer makes the one and only successful bid and isn't a practice used in Britain. Despite this, the misuse of the name is widespread and, for convenience, we'll continue to misuse it here. Curiously, builders and developers often refuse to take part in a Dutch auction when asked to review their offers, because vendors might try to push up the bidding and since negotiations are held in private, there's scope for sharp practice. The advantage of a Dutch auction is that offers are in the open and negotiations which involve naming other bids sometimes mean you can end by paying less than your maximum figure.

CONTRACTS RACES

When two or more acceptable offers are made, a vendor can select the successful buyer through a contracts race, which involves his solicitor issuing draft contracts to the bidders and the first to exchange contracts gets the plot. If a vendor suggests a contracts race, discuss this immediately with your solicitor. You must understand any risks involved in speeding matters up and be prepared to pay abortive fees if you lose. If you have doubts about a contracts race, and especially if you don't want to write off legal fees, don't enter.

CHANGING YOUR OFFER

After your offer is accepted and before you exchange contracts, you might come across a problem that means you're no longer willing to pay the agreed price. The scope for reducing your offer and still buying the plot depends largely on whether the reason for the reduction is personal to you, such as problems with finance, or applies to any purchaser, such as the need for special foundations. Personal reasons won't sway the vendor, unless you're the only buyer in a very quiet market. In these circumstances you might try lowering your offer, especially if you can sweeten the pill with an early date for exchange and completion. In a busy market, reducing your offer for personal reasons is likely to lose you the plot.

If you have good reasons that would apply to any purchaser, put the facts together before speaking to the agents. For example, an unmarked private sewer across the plot is discovered which must be diverted before building takes place. You would first need to assess whether it's a problem for the vendor to sort out before the sale continues or whether it's something that you would have to deal with as part of the construction. If it's something you would take on, get a written quote for the costs involved and then speak to the vendor or agents. Unless several thousand pounds is involved, the vendor would probably expect you to bear the extra cost. If the sum is significant and affects the plot's value, decide whether you can pay some part of it. Whatever the state of the market, approach reducing your offer carefully - by this stage you've put a good deal of effort into buying the plot and tact and some flexibility could help you keep it.

As we've seen, exchange of contracts is a legally binding agreement to buy. Don't sign the contract until you're satisfied with the results of all your investigations. It's not unusual for exchange of contracts to be delayed by a few days or even weeks, while problems are sorted out. Keep the agents informed of any difficulties and be as precise as you can about the problem and how long it'll take to sort out. Provided you maintain the agents' confidence in your ability and intention to go ahead, a delay in signing contracts shouldn't jeopardise your purchase.

GAZUMPING

Gazumping means that a vendor agrees a sale with one person but, before contracts are exchanged, accepts a higher offer from someone else. He is legally entitled to do this, despite any moral arguments against it. Some vendors, for example trustees or liquidators, are legally bound to consider any higher offer they get. Agents have a legal duty to their client, the vendor, to pass on offers even after a sale is agreed. You're particularly at risk of being gazumped if, for whatever reason, the vendor isn't confident in your ability to complete the sale. This lack of confidence usually manifests itself in continued marketing after the sale has been agreed. Check that any 'for sale' board is replaced by a 'sold subject to contract' sign, and that all advertising stops. If you're gazumped, decide whether it's worth making a higher offer or matching the other offer. Where your purchase is well under way, the vendor is likely to stick with you rather than start again from scratch.

Otherwise reaffirm to the agents that you remain interested in the plot, that your solicitor can act quickly and that your offer remains on the table. Ask the agents to let you know if the other purchaser doesn't complete. If the new purchaser drops out, there's then a good chance that your offer will be snapped up without further marketing of the plot. Most sales do go ahead though, so keep looking for another plot.

CHAPTER 19
AUCTIONS

Sales of plots by auction are more common in England and Wales than in Scotland and almost unheard of in Northern Ireland. They're well worth investigating, however, especially if you're looking for a bargain. There are differences between sale by auction and sale by private treaty and you must be clear about these before bidding for a plot at auction.

The first and most important point to understand about buying a plot by auction is that the fall of the auctioneer's hammer creates a binding contract. This equates to exchange of contracts in a sale by private treaty. Once the hammer has fallen, the sale progresses to completion in the normal way. Auction procedure is shown in Figure 19.1.

Before bidding at an auction, adequate preparation is essential. Your solicitor must have carried out all the searches and investigations of the title. Only then can you buy with confidence. Your investigations will be simplified as both the selling agent and the vendor's solicitors

AUCTION SALE PROCEDURE

YOU	SOLICITOR
INVESTIGATION *Check suitability of plot, planning permission, services, ground conditions.*	
INSTRUCT SOLICITOR *Give solicitor auction particulars and conditions of sale and address of your lender*	**INITIAL WORK** *Makes enquiries and inspects contract and title documents, carries out searches, contacts your lender*
COMPLETE RESEARCH *Read solicitor's report, calculate your maximum bid, have funds to cover deposit ready*	**REPORT** *Reports to you on: ownership, replies to enquiries, result of searches and contract*
AUCTION *Bid for plot, sign memorandum of sale, pay deposit, give solicitor's address, inform your solicitor*	**CONVEYANCE** *Prepares conveyance or transfer*
PURCHASE MONEY *You or your lender provide money for balance of purchase price*	**COMPLETION** *Pays over money in return for ownership documents*
POSSESSION *The plot becomes yours and you take over responsibility for it, pay your solicitor*	**REGISTRATION** *Pays stamp duty and registers the land in your name with HM Land Registry*

Figure 19.1

anticipate enquiries and should be geared up to answer them. Auction particulars are more detailed than ordinary sales particulars, including addresses of local councils and service authorities and information about easements and covenants. Particulars include a memorandum of sale and special conditions of sale (see Figure 19.2). The memorandum is for the successful buyer to sign as proof of purchase. The special conditions of sale set out details of the title and any restrictions; other documents, like the planning permission, should be available from the agent.

Tell your solicitors or conveyancers as soon as you're certain that you want to bid. They must liaise with the vendor's solicitors and carry out the necessary searches. You also need to make sure that your finance is in place. Even though, at this stage, you don't know whether you'll be successful in buying the plot, you still have to pay the solicitor and give a good deal of time and effort to your research. Don't think about bidding at auction unless you're certain that the plot is right for you. Where time is short or assessing the plot is complex, get professional help from a firm of surveyors. Explain the time pressures and make it absolutely clear what you need from them.

There's nothing to stop you making an offer for a plot before the auction. Because of the costs agents incur when arranging an auction (advertising, hire of hall, etc), they might be reluctant to entertain early offers but are, nevertheless, obliged to pass them on to their clients, unless given specific instructions to the contrary. Particulars marked 'for sale by auction unless previously sold', suggest a willingness, even an intention, to sell before the auction. An early offer has the disadvantage of indicating the amount that you're likely to bid at the auction and the vendor might adjust the reserve price. If you want to make an offer before the auction, do so as soon as the agents are instructed to sell. At this point, the agents haven't committed much time to arranging the auction and so might recommend the vendor to accept an early offer. You can put forward an offer at any time up to and including the day of the auction. The agents should have some idea of how many people are likely to bid and if there are very few, your offer might succeed.

EXAMPLE OF CONDITIONS ATTACHED TO AUCTION SALE PARTICULARS

GENERAL CONDITIONS OF SALE

1 The Vendors solicitors are Messrs Canister Coniston Blowfish of 49 Church Road, Hoopley, Muddlesex, GF4 1TH 01743 094635.

2 (a) The property is sold subject to the following conditions and to the conditions known as the National Conditions of Sale so far as the latter conditions are not inconsistent with these general and special conditions which are to prevail in case of any conflict.

(b) The prescribed rate of iending interest referred to in condition (4) of the National Conditions of Sale shall be 5% above the minimum ending rate of National Westminster Bank for the time being.

(c) A copy of the said conditions may be inspected at the offices of the auctioneers or of the solicitors for the Vendors on any day during business hours and in the sale room immediately before the sale and the purchaser shall be deemed to have full knowledge thereof.

3 Immediately following the sale the purchaser will pay a deposit of 10% of the purchase money to the auctioneers as stakeholders and shall sign the agreement hereinafter appearing.

4 Unless otherwise stated the sale is subject to a reserve price and the Vendors reserve the right to bid themselves or through their agents at the auction and to sell all or any part of the property by private treaty prior to the auction.

5 Notwithstanding anything in these conditions or in the particulars of sale no representation, warranty or condition whatsoever shall be made or implied howsoever arising either as to the state or condition of the property or any part thereof or as to whether the same is subject to any resolutions, schemes, development orders, notices or proposals of any sort whatsoever and the purchaser shall be deemed to purchase in all respects subject thereto and shall not be entitled to raise any requisition in respect thereof.

6 The auctioneers reserve the right (without assigning any reason therefore) in their sole absolute discretion to refuse to accept a bid.

SPECIAL CONDITIONS OF SALE

1 Vacant possession shall be given on completion.

2 Completion shall take place on the 13th day of May, 2009, at the office of the Vendor's solicitor.

3 Title shall commence with a Conveyance on sale dated 15th June 1947, and made between Richard Stanley Withers and William James Horns and the prior title shall in no circumstances be required or investigated.

4 The property is sold subject to but with the benefit of the provisions of a Deed of Grant dated 9th January 1984 whereby a right of way over the access road was granted by the owner or owners for the time being of Honeywood Cottage being the property immediately to the north. A copy of this Deed is available for inspection at the office of the auctioneers and of the Vendor's solicitors.

Figure 19.2

Figure 19.3

A small house on a large plot put into an auction sale in order to test the market

An auction is sometimes a last resort method of selling a plot, so you should first find out whether there's a problem and why any previous attempts to sell it were unsuccessful. Of course, not all plots sold in this way have something wrong with them. Trustees frequently sell properties at auctions, indicated in the particulars by a phrase like 'to be sold by order of trustees or executors'. Some plots are so special that their values are hard to predict and they're put into auctions to get the highest possible price through competitive bidding. In the latter cases, the plot normally goes to the auction no matter what offers are made beforehand.

There's a mystique surrounding auctions but the procedure for selling a plot is straightforward and the proceedings aren't difficult to follow. If the prospect of bidding alarms you, attend another auction to see at first hand how it's done or employ someone to bid for you. You don't need special inside knowledge to be able to buy a plot at auction.

The auctioneer doesn't set out at an incoherent gabble and bidding is usually made by clearly raising a hand. The auctioneer responds by repeating the figure bid before going on to seek the next bid.

In the auction room, there might be many people present. Not all will be buyers - some could be members of the auctioneer's staff, drafted in to create a busy atmosphere, other buyers have their solicitors or other professionals with them, inquisitive locals and neighbours also attend. A large crowd can disguise only a few genuine purchasers.

When the auction begins, the auctioneer first explains who he is and introduces the vendor's solicitor. As each property, or lot, comes up, the auctioneer gives a brief description and mentions any key documents, like the planning permission and points out items in the special conditions of sale, such as a restrictive covenant or right of way across the plot. The auctioneer states when completion is to take place and asks for any questions. Don't be dismayed if at this point someone stands up and asks loudly about some problem with the site, like a public footpath across it. If your thorough investigations haven't uncovered any problems, it's probably a buyer's ploy to discourage others from bidding. Where buyers make a public misrepresentation about a plot and then succeed in the auction, their contract could be void. Even if they don't succeed, they could still be liable for damages. Don't let this deter you from asking a genuine question, however.

The bidding is started by the auctioneer naming a figure, which might be low to encourage bidding or high but then rapidly reduced, to give the impression that a bargain is to be had. Vendors can reserve the right to bid themselves and in practice this usually means that the auctioneer bids on their behalf, taking imaginary bids or bids 'off the wall' as it's known. The particulars state whether a vendor reserves the right to bid. Bidding goes on until the reserve price is reached. This is the minimum sale price which the vendor and auctioneer agree before the auction and, if bids fail to reach this level, the lot is withdrawn. Once bids reach the reserve price, the auctioneer says that the lot 'is to be sold' or that bids are 'in the room'. Where bidding is brisk, the auctioneer might delay making this announcement until there's a pause, when it can help to get bidding moving again.

Once you know that the reserve has been reached, and thus the plot will be sold, your task is to secure it at the best possible figure. Keep in mind both the highest figure you can pay and your estimate of market value. You must judge exactly how far you're prepared to go. If bidding is moving in stages of £1,000 and you're within £3,000 or £4,000 of your limit, perhaps, slow your bids right down. The auctioneer can tell when buyers are nearing their ceiling figures and might then ask for bids in stages of, say, £500. If he doesn't, you can make such a bid yourself, by naming a figure as opposed to signalling your agreement to the one the auctioneer is seeking. The auctioneer might not accept the bid and by doing this you send a clear signal to other bidders that you're reaching your limit. If you accidentally make a bid beyond your limit, you can withdraw it before the fall of the hammer. Don't get carried away. Remember that, if the hammer falls after your bid, you're legally bound to buy.

If you're successful, you'll sign a memorandum of sale and pay a deposit, usually 10 per cent of the sale figure. You'll be asked where copies of the title deeds should be sent, so have your solicitor's name and address with you.

When a plot fails to reach its reserve, you can still try to buy it after the auction. Where bidding stops just short of the reserve, the vendor might negotiate, if he has set his figure too high. Tell the auctioneer that you want to make an offer. If the plot is bought after the auction, you can sign the memorandum of sale and pay the deposit as if the deal had been done in the auction or it could proceed as a private treaty sale.

CHAPTER 20 TENDERS

In England, Wales and Northern Ireland, formal tenders are rarely used to sell single plots but in Scotland tenders are the normal way of buying and selling plots and houses. In this chapter we first examine the special features of buying land in Scotland and then look at buying by formal tender generally.

BUYING A PLOT IN SCOTLAND

Scotland has a different legal system from the rest of Britain and different procedures for conveyancing and land registration, so you must use a solicitor who is a member of the Scottish Law Society. Scottish solicitors are more active in the property market than their counterparts elsewhere in Britain and act as both legal and property advisers.

When plots are put up for sale, the normal procedure is for offers to be invited over a given figure, which really does mean over, say, 10 - 15 per cent, or even more in a rising market. A closing date is given for offers to be made.

When you find a plot you want to

FORMAL TENDER PROCEDURE

YOU	SOLICITOR
INVESTIGATION *Check suitability of plot, planning permission, services and ground conditions*	
INSTRUCT SOLICITOR *Give solicitor tender particulars, and conditions of sale and address of your lender*	**INITIAL WORK** *Makes enquiries and inspects contract and title documents; carries out searches, contacts your lender*
COMPLETE TENDER *Read solicitor's report, calculate your offer, fill in tender form, enclose deposit and send to vendor's agent*	**REPORT** *Reports to you on: ownership, replies to enquiries, result of searches and contract*
ACCEPTANCE *Vendor's agent or solicitor sends you Form of Acceptance, if you are successful, inform your solicitor*	**CONVEYANCE** *Prepares conveyance or transfer*
PURCHASE MONEY *You or your lender provide money for balance of purchase price*	**COMPLETION** *Pays over money in return for ownership documents*
POSSESSION *The plot becomes yours and you take over responsibility for it, pay your solicitor*	**REGISTRATION** *Pays stamp duty and registers the land in your name with HM Land Registry*

Figure 20.1

buy, consult your solicitors about what would be the right offer. They'll advise on value and draft and submit the offer on your behalf. An offer is made as a sealed bid which, if accepted by the vendor, is termed conclusion of missives. This creates a binding contract and the sale moves ahead quickly with completion taking place in as little as a week. This is largely due to the relative simplicity of making title searches in Scotland, where there's a central register of property transactions.

Not all plot sales in Scotland are conducted by sealed bids nor is every property sold by solicitors. Estate agents are active in commercial and agricultural property and increasingly in the residential market too. Sales of land do take place by private treaty. If you're in any doubt about the method of sale, ask the agent or solicitor selling the plot or take advice from your own solicitor. Because offers can be binding when accepted, and sales move quickly, you must make all your investigations into the plot before you commit yourself to buy.

FORMAL TENDERS

We've already looked at the use of informal tenders as a way of seeking offers before contracts are agreed and signed. A formal tender is an offer to buy a plot which, if accepted, results in a binding contract. This method of sale favours vendors, as there's no scope for negotiation, rather than buyers, who incur legal and other costs in preparing their bid regardless of the outcome. For these reasons, formal tenders are normally used only in busy market conditions. The main stages are set out in Figure 20.1.

Preparing for a tender is the same as preparing for an auction. Tender particulars and conditions of sale received from the selling agent give the time and place for submitting your tender and you should pass this on to your solicitor immediately. All site investigations, enquiries and legal searches need to be carried out before your tender is submitted. Finance must be in place and a deposit cheque (normally for 10 per cent of your tender figure) has to be included with your tender. Read the conditions of sale carefully as they include conditions for tendering and probably rule out offers made subject to planning or subject to anything else. If you have doubts about any aspects of the plot, don't submit a tender.

When deciding on a figure for your tender, remember that this is your one and only bid, so make your best

EXAMPLE FORM OF TENDER COMPLETED BY A PROSPECTIVE PLOT PURCHASER

FORM OF TENDER

The Conditions of Tender and Sale should be read before completion and submission of this Form.

Tender to purchase the freehold land and buildings at London Road, Blankney, in the County of Midshire ('the property') in accordance with the conditions of Tender and Sale annexed hereto,

TO: Hellsteeth Farms Limited
c/o Messrs Gruff Jangle and Partners
Prospect House
Station Street
Bruntstop-on-Sticks
Midshire KM3 9FW

I/WE: MR & MRS K R BRAZEN
23 BOSTOCK DRIVE
CRESTFELL
MIDSHIRE
KM16 7MN

hereby offer to purchase the Property from Hellsteeth Farms Limited for the sum of:

SIXTY SIX THOUSAND AND FIVE HUNDRED POUNDS (£66,000)

and agree that this Form of Tender with written notice of acceptance signed on behalf of Hellsteeth Farms Limited and despatched by guaranteed next day delivery post on or before the 5th day of August 2009 to me/us at my/our above mentioned address shall form a binding contract and subject to the Conditions of Tender and Sale. A Bankers Draft in favour of Fripp Holdstight and Barrier for ten per centum of the sum tendered is enclosed.

Dated this 1st day of August 2009

Signature/signatures Kelvin Brazen

Address of Agent or of Principal where different from above:

....

Name and Address of Tenderer's Solicitors:
PULLET SCUTTLE & CO, CRANSTOCK PLACE, BRUNTSTOP-ON-STICKS KM5 2RD

NOTES:
When submitting this Form of Tender, please ensure you comply with the Conditions of Tender, that the form is correctly filled in, and the Banker's Draft is in the right amount and payable to the Vendor's Solicitor. Do not submit the Tender unless you are certain you can proceed with the purchase, if successful.

Figure 20.2

BUYING YOUR PLOT CHECK LIST

- Be ready to act quickly once you find a plot you want to buy; get a letter from your lender or bank confirming the availability of funds
- Discuss the plot with the agent/vendor and make your offer
- Get answers to all your queries before you exchange contracts
- Before bidding at an auction or submitting a tender your solicitor must have checked ownership documents and you must be satisfied you can build your house on it
- Check that sale plans agree with the plot boundaries on the ground and get the plot pegged out, if necessary
- Make sure you understand fully all the implications of an option or conditional contract
- Stay in touch with the agent/ vendor throughout the purchase
- When you buy a plot, don't start work until you have detailed planning permission and building regulations approval

offer. Try to get an indication from the vendor's agents of what they think the market value is and what level the vendor might accept. There's little point in attempting to save money by putting in a figure below your best, merely because the vendor's agents claim that a lower figure might be acceptable. Get professional help if you're determined to buy the plot but don't have enough time to carry out the necessary research thoroughly. When you fill in the tender document make sure that all the details are correct and double check that everything is presented in the way specified, as failure to do this can invalidate your tender (see Figure 20.2). Enclose your deposit cheque correctly filled in, signed and dated. Tender particulars state where to send your tender, usually to either the vendor's agents or solicitors. There might be instructions on how to mark the envelope, or even a special envelope provided, but if not, mark it 'Tender Documents' and the name of the property.

Developers often time the submission of their tenders carefully and some send them by messenger, who loiters outside the agents' office until five minutes before the time limit. This is done to minimise the risk of sharp practice, as a dishonest agent could open tenders early and pass on information to another buyer. If you want to be safe, you could deliver the tender yourself, on the morning of the tender date; otherwise send it by registered mail and telephone to check that it has arrived.

If you're successful in your tender, the agents will let you know that your tender has been accepted, subject to clearance of your deposit cheque. A formal notice is sent by the vendor's solicitors and the purchase goes on to completion in the normal way. If you're unsuccessful, you'll be informed and your deposit cheque returned. You'll no doubt be interested in the amount of the successful tender but the agents are unlikely to tell you. They'll normally say how many tenders there were and roughly where you came in the pecking order. This is useful information as it gives you a clearer picture of the level of competition for the type of plot you're seeking.

PART 6 CASE STUDIES

Successfully finding and buying a plot of land to build your house on, or a property to convert, is as much about your personal qualities as it is about technical knowledge. Persistence, ingenuity, forward planning, flexibility, imagination and bare-faced cheek can all play a vital role in land-finding. The first five Parts of this book give you the knowledge and information you'll need. In this final Part, we see how three couples have put this all together - the challenges they faced, the methods they used and the valuable lessons learned which they want to pass on to you.

CASE STUDY 1 JOHN & BARBARA COOK

John and Barbara lived in a flat on the sea front and wanted to move to something larger. Having looked around unsuccessfully for a suitable property, they decided the only way to get exactly what they wanted was to build their own house. Having made this decision, the Cooks carried out a lot of research into all aspects of building your own home so they knew what they wanted to achieve and how, and what would be involved at each stage of the project. John and Barbara both had businesses in the town where they currently lived and so didn't want to build very far away. The first step was to register with three of four local estate agents, to go out looking for sites themselves and to make sure that all their friends and contacts knew they were in the market for land. Plots were around in their area but John and Barbara were looking for the right sort of location for the house they wanted to create. They also got their finances sorted out so that the funds to purchase a

Figure 21.1

John and Barbara's plot being cleared for building

plot were in place to enable them to move quickly, when the right opportunity came up.

One day while driving around their area of search, the Cooks spotted a 'for sale' board of an agent they hadn't registered with – the site was in a good location and looked interesting. John rang the agent. Unfortunately, he was told that the plot had sold. Out of interest, John and Barbara went to see the site anyway. The property had been a smithy but the blacksmith had retired and the site had been rundown and was now becoming overgrown. The land was about 36 metres (120 feet) deep by 27 metres (90 feet) wide and, being on a hillside, sloped slightly but benefited from good views. The property was outside the developed area where the council normally allowed new houses to be built but, because the site had an established commercial use, which ceased only a year ago, outline planning permission for one dwelling had been given. They liked the site

John and Barbara's house nearing completion

very much but it had been sold and so that was that. However, John and Barbara asked the estate agent to let them know if any similar plots came on their books.

A short while later the same agent did ring the Cooks to say the sale had fallen through and the smithy plot was back on the market. John and Barbara quickly considered their position and decided they would go for the site and worked out a price to put forward. They rang the agent back to make their offer. To their dismay, they had been pipped to the post by one hour – the one other person interested in the plot had beaten them to it. John and Barbara had missed the ideal plot for a second time. However, somehow or other destiny seemed to be on their side and the second potential purchaser wasn't able to complete as he didn't have the necessary funds in place. John and Barbara reiterated their offer and the vendor, no doubt somewhat fed up with the process by now, said he would accept the offer provided the Cooks could complete the purchase within one month. While the purchase was under way, they went in to the council's offices to talk to the planning officer about the site. The council confirmed it wanted to see only one house on the site and John and Barbara established that the type of house they had in mind was likely to be accepted by the council. Since funds were already in place, John and Barbara instructed a solicitor and the purchase did go through within the month requested by the vendor.

Having completed the purchase, the Cooks had four test holes dug by a digger and commissioned a report by a soil engineer. Fortunately, the ground conditions were favourable. John and Barbara made a planning application for the design they wanted – a traditional style brick and block house with four bedrooms, totalling 2,500 square feet. This went through without problems and construction went ahead. The result is a successful project with John and Barbara living in a house that meets their requirements exactly, in a good location close to their businesses and friends.

JOHN & BARBARA'S TOP TIPS

- find the right location – it's no good putting your ideal home on the wrong site
- check there's a planning permission that would allow you to build what you want
- make sure you have money in place so there's no hold up when you find a plot

CASE STUDY 2

GEOFF & SHARON JONES

Geoff and Sharon had already built one house for themselves five or six years ago, clearing their mortgage in the process. Geoff had left his job and was looking for something new to get involved in. The idea started to form that he could become a 'house-husband', in the sense that he could stay at home building a new house while Sharon continued to work to support them. The Jones were just thinking about this but hadn't made a decision to look again when one day Geoff was out and about driving and spotted a 'for sale' board outside a house and barns for conversion. He drove straight to the estate agents to get the particulars. Unfortunately, the house and barns were being sold as one lot, which put the property out of their reach. However, since no one came forward to buy the property on that basis, the seller decided to split the house and barn and sell them separately. Geoff and Sharon made an appointment to view the barns. There was a large and a small barn, which would

Figure 213

Sharon, Geoff and their daughter, Penny, outside their partially converted barn

convert to form a 3,500 square foot house, and other attached structures to be removed, set in a site of just under 0.40 hectares (one acre). The guide price was offers in the region of £70,000 and, because of the level of interest, the seller decided to ask for sealed bids. Geoff and Sharon thought about what the barns would be worth to them and put that figure at £75,000. They thought that, being a round figure, others might go in at the same amount and chose to add a couple of thousand just to make sure. In the event the vendor didn't accept the highest bid but rather went for the one who said he could proceed quickly – the successful bidder said he had the money ready whereas Geoff and Sharon had a house to sell. They asked the agent to let them know if the barns came back on the market and went away very disappointed.

Going through the episode with the barns had, at least, made Geoff and Sharon realise they definitely wanted to do something and they began an active search.

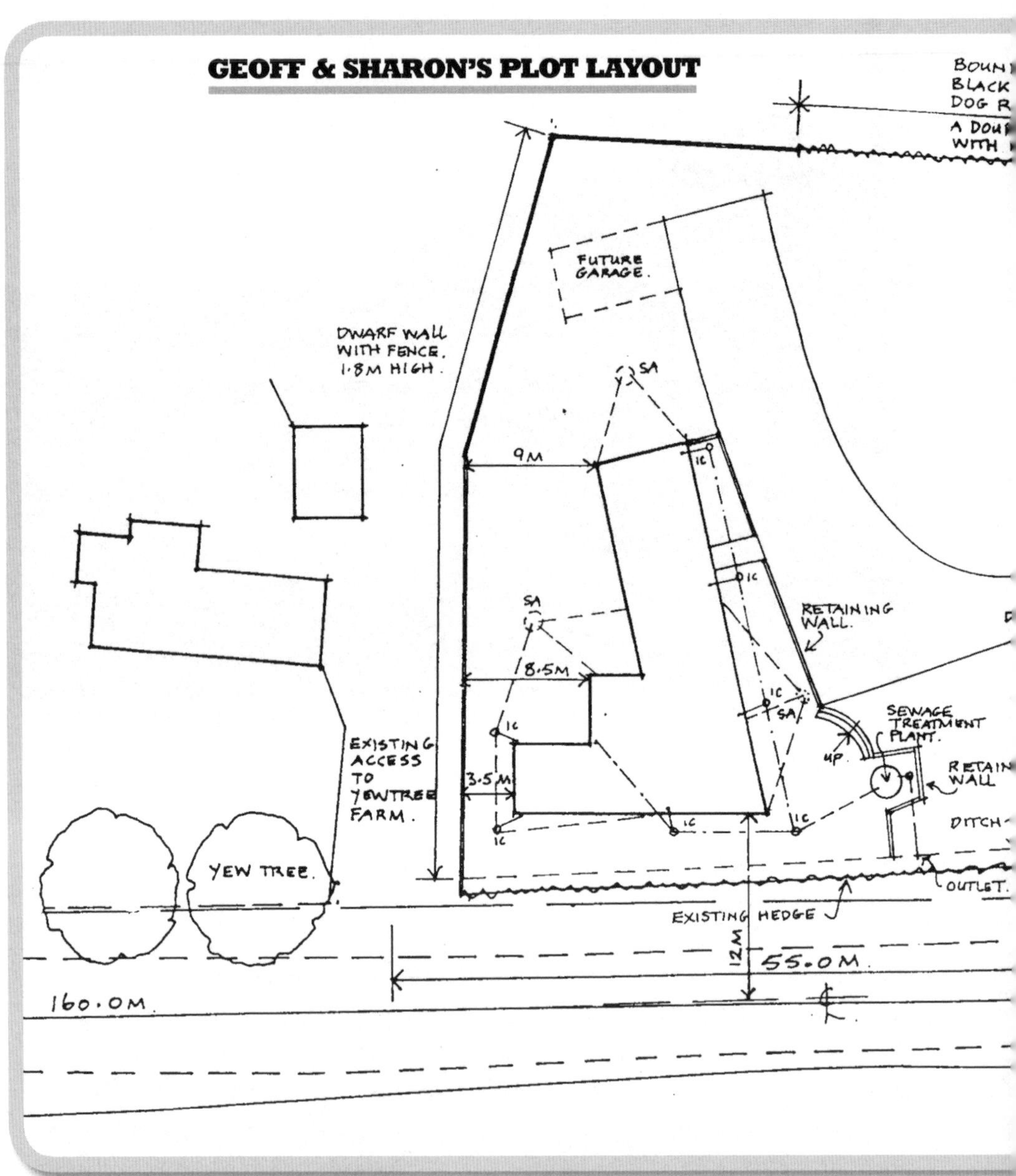

They drove around the area looking for opportunities, looked in local newspapers and shop windows, and put the word out at work and amongst their friends. Geoff and Sharon did register with estate agents, giving them a fairly open brief, which proved too much for

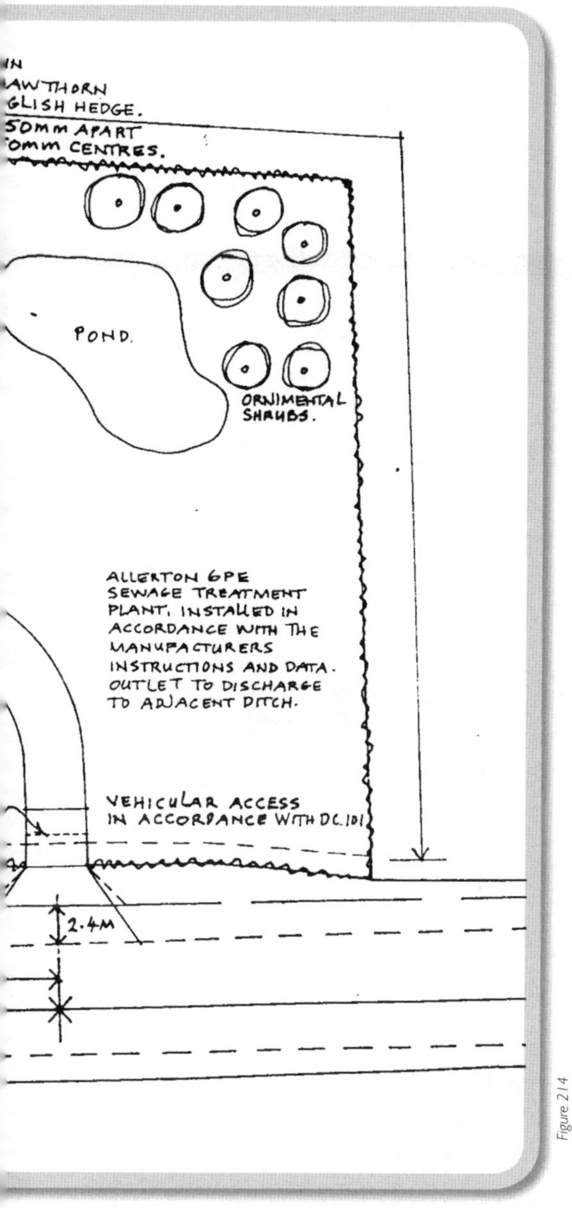

Figure 214

the agents to handle because all they sent out was the one thing Geoff and Sharon didn't want - bungalows in the wrong locations.

Geoff and Sharon were flexible in what sort of project they would take on. They looked at a row of cottages that had been converted 100 years ago, a 1950s house needing much work and a pair of damp and rotten cottages, one of which hadn't been lived in for years, the other was more recently vacated and the dividing garden wall between the two was made of old freezers. Geoff and Sharon thought the pair of cottages would be worth about £60,000 yet the asking price was £105,000. Prices in the area were starting to move up.

Whilst there were opportunities around, Geoff and Sharon were looking at the local paper contemplating placing an advert for plots when they saw the barns they had lost being re-advertised. They telephoned the agent. The sale that had been agreed six months ago had fallen fall through because, as it turned out, the prospective purchaser hadn't been a cash buyer. The agent hadn't contacted Geoff and Sharon as requested. The Jones' increased their offer to £80,000 but the agent said the owner wouldn't accept as he wanted more. Geoff responded saying his best offer was £85,000 and the vendor had until the end of the week to accept it. Meanwhile, having doubts about the information coming form the agent, Sharon went to see the farmer selling the house and he remembered her from the previous round of marketing. He agreed to accept Geoff and Sharon's offer and to wait while they sold their house. Geoff and Sharon put their house on the market and got a buyer but, while the sale was going through, he dropped out. Fortunately, a second buyer came along quickly and the sale progressed.

At the same time, Geoff and Sharon carried out checks on the barns. There was already a planning permission and they spoke to the architect, who gave his permission for his design to be used. The architect also said that his structural engineer colleague didn't believe the barns would need underpinning (in due course, this proved not to be the case). The sale of the Jones' house took three months to complete and they kept up the pressure on the solicitors to keep things moving. Unfortunately, the search which had been carried out when the first sale fell through was now over six months old and so a new search had to be carried out. At last everything went through – they had got their barns. With their house sold, Geoff and Sharon arranged a mobile home for the site, got drainage laid on, a domestic electricity supply connected and put their furniture into storage. Knowing this would be their last chance for a few years, Geoff, Sharon and their daughter, Penny, went to America on holiday for a month before rolling up their sleeves and getting stuck into the conversion.

GEOFF & SHARON'S TOP TIPS

- immerse yourself in the market – get a feel for values, locations and what's coming up
- be open-minded – look at conversion, renovation and new-build
- don't rely on estate agents – short circuit the system when it doesn't work
- follow up on properties that you miss first time round

CASE STUDY 3

KEN & PAT SKINNER

Ken and Pat enjoyed DIY but wanted to take things a stage further and design their own home to create the space exactly as they wanted it. They originally thought of building a cottage-style house but, having converted their existing home from an old school, decided they wanted to go contemporary. Ken and Pat had been considering building for years but the point came at the beginning the year to get serious. They had no preference for a type of plot although didn't really want a typical garden plot and, ideally, wanted land but realised this would be expensive. Ken and Pat were well established in the area where they lived so didn't want to buy more than 10-15 miles away. They had about £80,000 available to spend on a plot and £120,000 for the construction. Ken's job involves travelling around the area so he kept his eyes open while out and about. The Skinners didn't fancy being bothered by estate agents so searched agents' websites for plots and scoured local papers. This

Figure 215

The 'for sale' board which first caught Ken's eye

gave them a feel for the local plot market and prices. They were keen to purchase and found they had to resist the temptation to jump at every plot they came across.

While travelling to a job, Ken saw a board on a site 15 minutes from their home. On the next trip past he stopped to have a look. The plot was part of a former railway line, next to where the station had been many years ago, fairly close to the centre of a village. Ken's first impression was the site might be too large – the agents' board said 'development site'. He went on-line to find out more and discovered there was outline permission for two detached houses but no asking price, just offers invited. Ken phoned the agent to be told the site was being sold by the county council which wanted to sell the land as a whole. However, it transpired the site had been on the market for a while, the guide price was £250,000 and the main interest was from a builder who wanted to buy one plot first and the other later on. Seizing the initiative, Ken asked, if the seller was prepared to consider that, would

Figure 216

Ken and Pat's plot is a good size and in a spacious edge-of-village setting

it sell him one plot. Ken went back to the site with Pat and they both had a good feeling about the land which was enhanced when they discovered it adjoined a nature reserve. Ken and Pat preferred the eastern plot as a footpath adjoined the other one. The eastern plot was about 0.10 hectares (0.25 acres), mainly overgrown with a line of mature lime trees towards the middle of the site.

Within a few days of seeing the plot, knowing what plots fetched locally and conscious of his rough budget, Ken and Pat phoned the agent with an initial offer of £90,000 which wasn't accepted. The vendor was looking for £115,000 for each plot. Ken and Pat reconsidered and went back with an offer of £105,000. After a week the answer came back that the seller had accepted.

The agent provided the addresses of the service suppliers. Ken phoned each of them to check availability of connections and all said this shouldn't be a problem. He got a quote for water supply connection which was £1,600. News came through that the adjoining plot had been sold to a builder so Ken contacted him and they agreed to co-ordinate over getting services laid on. The division between the two plots and the land to the rear which the county council also owned weren't fenced but the seller had had the site measured and boundaries marked. Ken and Pat investigated the planning situation, arranging a meeting with a planning officer to discuss the sort of house they wanted. They took a sketch Ken had drawn and a computer generated image of a package company's design similar to the style they were thinking of. Ken and Pat were pleased at the positive response from the officer who couldn't see a problem for the proposed size and design. Ken also looked at the file on the planning application which he found very informative. Amongst other things, it contained a detailed report by the tree officer which said none of the trees was valuable.

They arranged to meet the tree officer at the property to discuss felling some trees to open up the site more. The planning permission included a requirement to widen the road next to the plot and construct a pavement. This would eat into the plot slightly but it was deep enough to accommodate that without affecting layout unduly. Ken lined up his draughtsman step son to draw up his design and started preparing his planning application so it could be submitted as soon as the deal completed.

There was some delay over the transaction going through, while the vendor sorted itself out, but Ken and Pat loved the plot and were satisfied it would be the perfect spot for them to create the home they dreamed of for years.

KEN & PAT'S TOP TIPS

- Don't rush into buying the first plot you see
- Get a feel for the area, have a good walk around the plot and imagine living there
- Don't be scared to make an offer on a plot for what you think it's worth - be bold
- A lot of people would love to buy a plot but are scared to go for it - if you have a dream try to make it come true

Index

N

O

P

R

S

T

U

V

W

THE AUTHORS

Michael Dade and Roy Speer are consultants, writers and speakers on planning and land matters. Both are Chartered Planning and Development Surveyors with degrees in Estate Management. They run their own specialist town and country planning practice, Speer Dade Planning Consultants, carrying out a wide range of work throughout the country for their book readers, individuals, builders/developers, landowners, businesses and other organisations. Their consultancy work includes making and advising on planning applications, appeals and enforcement, giving evidence at hearings and public inquiries, carrying out planning potential reports, and a useful, cost-effective advice-by-post service for readers.

Contact Roy Speer and Michael Dade
01273 843737 or 01825 890870
roy@speerdade.co.uk
mike@speerdade.co.uk
www.speerdade.co.uk